Praise for *The Fire That Makes Us*

"In *The Fire That Makes Us*, Dr. Jalali offers a compelling and compassionate exploration of the human journey from fragmentation to wholeness. Drawing on deep psychological insight and personal truth, this book speaks to the silent struggles so many carry—and does so with warmth, clarity, and hope. It is a powerful companion for those seeking meaning, healing, and transformation."

—**Sherri Mahdavi,** PhD, Jungian analyst

"In *The Fire That Makes Us*, Dr. Shahrzad Jalali masterfully intertwines her clinical expertise with narrative storytelling, offering readers an intimate exploration of personal transformation. Through the lens of Charlotte, a psychologist confronting her own unresolved grief and emotional complexities, Dr. Jalali delves into themes of love, loss, and self-discovery. Each chapter concludes with reflective insights, encouraging readers to engage in their own introspection and personal growth. This book is a testament to the power of self-awareness and the transformative journey toward healing."

—**Patricia Caldani,** professor of biology, University of La Verne

"Dr. Jalali's *The Fire That Makes Us* is one of the most compelling books I've read in recent years. In these pages, one finds a rare fusion of narrative depth and clinical insight. Within Dr. Jalali's deftly woven anecdotes, the story of Charlotte allows the reader to reflect on trauma and resilience. What makes this book stand out is the translation of clinical ideas into language that feels both grounded and genuinely human. Drawing on a Jungian foundation, Dr. Jalali does not prescribe quick fixes, instead she invites readers to engage with their experiences in a way that fosters long-term integration and meaning.

As a clinical psychologist, I appreciated how accurately she captures the internal conflicts many of our clients face: the push and pull between remembering and forgetting, connection and withdrawal, identity and avoidance. The sections on emotional pain, agency, and the role of values in recovery are particularly well done as they are deep without being abstract, practical without losing nuance. While this is not a clinical manual, *The Fire That Makes Us* offers something rarer: a sustained reflection on what it actually feels like to live with trauma and to move forward. It's a valuable read not only for therapists and clients, but for anyone interested in how people heal."

—**Sean Sterling,** PhD, ABPP, professor of applied clinical psychology at The Chicago School of Professional Psychology

The Fire That Makes Us

Unveiling the Transformative Power of Trauma

SHAHRZAD JALALI, PsyD

GREENLEAF
BOOK GROUP PRESS

This book is intended as a reference volume only. It is sold with the understanding that the publisher and author are not engaged in rendering any professional services. The information given here is designed to help you make informed decisions. If you suspect that you have a problem that might require professional treatment or advice, you should seek competent help.

Published by Greenleaf Book Group Press
Austin, Texas
www.gbgpress.com

Distributed by Greenleaf Book Group

For ordering information or special discounts for bulk purchases, please contact Greenleaf Book Group at PO Box 91869, Austin, TX 78709, 512.891.6100.

Design and composition by Greenleaf Book Group
Cover design by Greenleaf Book Group
Cover image © Maries Danila

Publisher's Cataloging-in-Publication data is available.

Print ISBN: 979-8-88645-348-5

eBook ISBN: 979-8-88645-349-2

To offset the number of trees consumed in the printing of our books, Greenleaf donates a portion of the proceeds from each printing to the Arbor Day Foundation. Greenleaf Book Group has replaced over 50,000 trees since 2007.

Printed in the United States of America on acid-free paper

25 26 27 28 29 30 31 32 10 9 8 7 6 5 4 3 2 1

First Edition

To Dr. Sherri Mahdavi,

With profound gratitude for your unwavering guidance and boundless wisdom. Your mentorship has been a beacon of light, illuminating not only the depths of my work but the expanse of my being. You have shaped my path with compassion and insight, leaving an indelible mark on my journey. This book, and the growth it represents, is as much a reflection of your influence as it is my own exploration. Thank you for teaching me the art of seeing and the courage to embrace the unseen.

Contents

Introduction

Have you ever felt that life, with all its chaos and complexity, is overwhelming and sometimes even meaningless? Do you sometimes find yourself on the brink of surrender, feeling that no matter how much effort you put forth, things never seem to align with your desires? Do lingering shadows of negative emotions follow you, despite your best attempts to chase them away?

Welcome to the shared journey of the human experience. Even if these sentiments don't resonate with you at this moment, it is almost certain that, at some point, you will find yourself navigating these turbulent waters.

You might think that these feelings are just the harsh realities of life, something we must all endure without hope of escape. But what if I told you there is another path—a path to processing emotions that fosters harmony instead of disintegration and fragmentation?

As a practicing clinical psychologist specializing in trauma and emotional resilience, my approach is deeply rooted in a Jungian orientation, exploring the profound influence of the unconscious on our life stories. This book is a testament to my dedication to guiding individuals on their paths of self-discovery and healing, drawing from both extensive clinical practice and my own personal journey.

My journey into psychology began not as a clinician but as a patient, navigating the intricate labyrinth of the unconscious mind and its emotional complexities. During a particularly tumultuous period, I sought therapy for the first time. This transformative experience ignited a passion within me, leading me to transition from an established career in linguistics to the study of psychology, ultimately becoming a clinician. This book is both a personal endeavor and a clinical amalgamation of my practice over the past decade, crafted to inspire others to discover the path that has profoundly helped me and countless patients I have worked with. It serves as a blueprint for navigating the major dichotomies of the human psyche.

The main character of this book, Charlotte, is a reflection of my personal experiences and the emotional challenges I've observed in my patients over the years. Her story serves as a beacon, guiding you to delve into your own inner turmoil and your relationship with it. Charlotte embodies the essence of how life's ebb and flow shape our moods, emotions, decisions, and—ultimately—our destinies. By learning to reframe our thoughts, feelings, and reactions, we discover the profound liberation that comes with transforming our own narratives.

Charlotte's journey, marked by significant trauma and inner struggles, mirrors the experiences of many. The intention here is not to dwell on the trauma itself, as we are all familiar with life's myriad pains, but to illuminate the inner work that leads to what in psychology we call integration. Integration is about weaving the threads of our experiences into a cohesive whole.

The purpose of this book is to provide a living example of how to create a roadmap to integration and apply it to your own inner turmoil. While self-help books, workshops, and seminars often provide tools and methods for alleviating psychological distress, the complexity of human emotions and their diverse manifestations calls for a more nuanced approach. By following Charlotte's journey, we will explore a step-by-step interpretation of psychological pain and discover means for addressing it.

Through Charlotte's story, I aim to offer a tangible representation of the inner work necessary for navigating life's challenges, demonstrating how integration—not necessarily resolution—of opposites can lead to a more coherent and fulfilling sense of self.

1

Remembering Versus Forgetting

The cold autumn morning coaxed Charlotte into staying indoors. Seated at her kitchen table, she savored her coffee. She caught sight of her reflection in the microwave and wiped away a small fleck of milk foam from her nose. The flicker of a genuine smile only served to unearth the lingering sadness within her. It made her feel guilty, as if she didn't deserve to smile after what she'd been through.

A tear traced down her left cheek, and she closed her eyes. Memories surged forward, transporting her back to the scene of the accident: Her face was wet, and she couldn't see anything. With only fragmented recollections of noise and fear and pain—a car crash—she tried to look around but couldn't get her eyes to open. The cacophony of noises and voices intensified to an unbearable level. Through the sensory overload, she realized she was on the roadside, but where were her parents? They had been with her in the car. Questions and confusion swirled in her mind.

The liquid continued to run down her face. She was extremely thirsty. In a desperate attempt to quench it, she parted her lips, expecting rainwater but instead tasting the metallic tang of blood. She was hurt. Fear gripped her. She thought, *What if I'm blind?* With trembling hands, she attempted to touch her eyes, but all she felt was intense swelling and raw flesh.

The terror paralyzed her until her mother's voice cut through the chaos: "What happened? Why are we here?"

Although Charlotte couldn't see her, the solace of her mother's voice provided a semblance of comfort. Patiently, Charlotte said, "We were on our way to the airport. We must have been in a car accident."

Seconds passed, and her mother repeated the exact same question. It dawned on Charlotte that her mother was delirious, possibly due to emotional distress or severe injuries. Regardless, all she could do was respond, repeating her answer tirelessly as her mom continued to ask the same question until they were pulled away from each other.

Despite having suffered a head injury, Charlotte felt alert. Each detail intensified, as if her mind was painting a vivid picture of the events around her, even in the absence of sight. She knew she had to ensure they were taken to a reputable hospital. She knew she had to make calls for help. She felt a hand touch her. She asked urgently, "Where are my parents? I can't hear them."

In response, the person withdrew their hand and replied coldly, "Let me do my work. They are in different ambulances."

Doubt gnawed at Charlotte. She remembered her mother's voice, affirming her survival, but where was her father?

Her phone buzzing on the marble kitchen counter jolted Charlotte back to the present. Sighing with relief, she realized she was safe and checked her phone. One of her patients had texted, requesting a change in their psychotherapy appointment for the following week. Charlotte surveyed the room, breathed deeply, and grounded herself in the present. However, a part of her remained trapped in the past. No matter how hard she tried, she couldn't escape the experiences that had shaped her.

To those who observed Charlotte, it would seem that she had successfully moved on from her past. However, deep inside, she often questioned the possibility of truly leaving it all behind. If moving on meant reengaging with life and fulfilling her responsibilities, then yes, she had managed to do so. But if moving on meant erasing the impact that her past trauma had on her identity, she found herself at a loss. The accident wasn't merely an event that had happened to her; it had altered the very core of who she was, and she struggled to comprehend how to reverse that change.

Charlotte responded to her patient's text and felt grateful to her patient for pulling her out of the unpleasant daydream. She finished her coffee and went to take a shower; she couldn't afford to spend her day dwelling on the past. Her life had been a tapestry of experiences, filled with moments of both joy and sorrow. It was a life characterized by various ups and downs, some of which she enjoyed revisiting and others she preferred to bury deep within her memory.

Charlotte had gained enough perspective to understand that every person's story encompasses ebbs and flows. During moments of clarity, she could even discern wisdom from her own personal falls. However, she also felt the weight of her losses. She judged herself harshly for her lingering emotions about the accident and numerous other aspects of her life. Deep down, she yearned to erase those experiences, to forget the person she had become, and to revert to her former self. Above all, she longed to regain the sense that everything would be all right. But now she knew better. She understood that the world could turn against her in an instant, and there was nothing she could do about it. She would have to make peace with reality and find a way to move forward.

Charlotte opened the window and was greeted by a breeze. As the crisp fall air cascaded over her, she questioned whether the experiences that had sculpted her could—or should—be forgotten. She oscillated between wanting to erase those memories and yearning to repeatedly mull over them. It felt crucial to revisit them, tumbling them like rocks in a river until the sharp edges were worn away.

Charlotte wondered, What if the lows in life held as much value as the highs? What if the unpredictability and inconsistency were intricately woven into the fabric of genuine joy? And what if relinquishing parts of her story meant forfeiting the potential for true delight? Was leaving the past behind her even possible?

The Struggle Between Holding On and Letting Go

Psychology offers a crucial intervention for individuals who have experienced a traumatic event that continues to inflict emotional pain. The objective of this trauma work is to reduce the emotional intensity associated with the perceived pain. Over the past few decades, various interventions have been developed to relieve emotional distress caused by trauma. However, among these efforts, a fundamental question arises: What truly happens to the memories? Can you genuinely forget and move on? Can the past really be undone? Can something so painful be truly forgotten?

When something or someone of significance is forgotten, it becomes detached from the psyche, which can itself be a traumatic experience. The goal of trauma work is not to help individuals forget what has caused them pain, but rather to redefine the meaning assigned to those experiences. Forgetting in some cases may be an unintended side effect of trauma work rather than the intended outcome.

On the other hand, remembering with ease can enable you to redefine your experiences from a more tolerable perspective, ultimately leading to healing. To alleviate the anguish you may be feeling from some traumatic event in your past, it helps to acknowledge the undesirable event and the burdens that may have followed it. In trauma work, you are provided with an opportunity to revisit memories while exploring avenues that were previously unavailable during the helplessness of the distressing event.

When you are going through a traumatic event, you are helpless and at the mercy of the situation and circumstances. Afterward, you can implement your power for redefining because you have survived the situation on some level. You can open up space to switch your perspective from being the victim of a traumatic event to being the survivor. That allows you to reconnect to your power rather than remaining in loss of power. Through this process, new neural pathways for coping with the trauma emerge, which are more welcoming and less distressing. The objective when confronting an unwanted memory is not necessarily to erase it but to recollect it in a less distressing manner.

Survivors of trauma often have fragmented memories of the event. This fragmented recall is a sensible response of the brain, aimed at protecting the survivor from further discomfort. Amnesia—forgetting the event entirely—associated with trauma also serves as a protective mechanism, shielding the psyche from reexperiencing the pain and stress associated with the traumatic occurrence. In the face of danger, the brain becomes hyperfocused on the immediate threat, inadvertently missing numerous details. Many individuals are troubled by these gaps in memory and feel the need to fill them in, to construct a coherent narrative and process the trauma effectively. Therapeutic interventions such as hypnosis can assist in retrieving lost fragments of memories; however, it is crucial to respect the psyche's choice to dissociate from certain information.

At times, missing information gradually resurfaces with the passage of time, enabling the survivor to process and digest it.

In other instances, the information remains inaccessible. Either way, genuine emotional processing of traumatic events is aided by interpreting the intact memories and assigning meaning to your experience.

Examine Your Feelings Around Trauma

Individuals suffering from post-traumatic stress disorder (PTSD) may exhibit an exaggerated response to the trauma that surpasses the actual intensity of the event. This phenomenon of heightened recall of trauma-related pain can be seen as a memory distortion, involving the formation of exaggerated sensational responses as a result of experiencing traumatic events. This exaggerated recall may be an adaptive response or a manifestation of the psyche's limitations in response to overwhelming emotional situations.

Regardless of the underlying cause, the important part is how we come to terms with these memories as part of our life story. What you remember is not as crucial as how you feel when those memories resurface. The goal of trauma work is to diminish the overwhelming emotional response and transform it into a more tolerable sensory experience. In simpler terms, what takes place with traumatic memories in therapy involves establishing a new, more tolerable association that contrasts with the exaggerated response formed during the traumatic event.

In trauma therapy, your primary objective is not to erase painful memories but to reinterpret and integrate these experiences in a less distressing manner. Trauma work focuses on reducing the emotional intensity of your traumatic memories by fostering new, more tolerable neural pathways for coping. This process involves acknowledging the traumatic event, exploring previously unavailable avenues for understanding it, and diminishing exaggerated emotional responses. Ultimately, the goal is to transform your relationship with your memories, allowing you to recall the events without overwhelming emotional distress, thereby promoting healing and improving your quality of life. By renegotiating your initial response to the trauma, you can redefine its impact on your life, making it more manageable and less painful over time.

As you could see in the previous segment, Charlotte continues to struggle, as she has not yet fully integrated the traumatic event and feels overwhelmed and overstimulated by it—as if the trauma continues to define her life. By renegotiating your initial response to the trauma, you can redefine its impact on your life, making it more manageable and less painful over time. Ultimately, the goal is to transform your relationship with your memories, allowing you to recall the events without feeling a sense of overwhelming emotional distress. This will promote healing.

Finding Ease in the Healing Process of Trauma

To begin the process of understanding and healing from trauma, start by tuning in to your emotional and physical responses as you recall the memories. What emotions arise when you reflect on the traumatic experience? Are you feeling sadness, anger, fear, or perhaps a mix of emotions?

Next, observe how your body responds to these memories. Do you notice any physical sensations or tensions, such as tightness in your chest, a knot in your stomach, or a racing heart? Paying attention to these bodily reactions can provide valuable insights into how your trauma is stored in both your mind and body. This awareness is the first step in processing and ultimately healing from the trauma.

By paying close attention to these reactions, it's possible to gain a deeper understanding of how the trauma continues to affect the present. This awareness is the first step in addressing and ultimately healing from the experience. Recognizing that the body and mind are reacting to a past event as if it's still occurring allows for the exploration of strategies to release this tension. Whether through therapy, mindfulness, or physical practices, this process can help in moving beyond the trauma.

The Effects of Trauma

Trauma's lasting effects often extend beyond physical injury, subtly influencing emotional and psychological well-being. While persistent physical discomfort is a known consequence, the emotional and psychological ramifications are equally pervasive, often manifesting in ways that subtly shape behavior and thought patterns.

For instance, long after a traumatic event, the body may react to specific triggers with tension, a racing heart, or an inexplicable sense of dread. These physical responses indicate the body's ongoing remembrance of trauma. Emotionally, trauma might lead to chronic anxiety, irritability, or a sense of unease, often disconnected from present circumstances but deeply rooted in past experiences.

Such responses may drive avoidance behaviors—steering clear of certain places, activities, or relationships—that limit life in ways not immediately obvious to you. For example, avoiding social situations due to anxiety might trace back to a past event where your safety was compromised, even if you don't consciously recognize the connection.

These patterns highlight the mind and body's intertwined response to trauma. Recognizing these signs is essential for healing, as it opens the door to exploring therapeutic methods that address and resolve the lingering effects, ultimately fostering a return to balance and well-being.

The emotional impact of trauma can manifest in various ways, often intertwining with everyday life in complex patterns. For example, trauma can lead to overwhelming fear and anxiety, as seen in someone who becomes terrified of driving after a car accident, developing a generalized anxiety that permeates many aspects of daily life. This anxiety might be accompanied by depression, marked by persistent sadness, hopelessness, and a loss of interest in activities they once enjoyed. To manage these distressing emotions, the person may sometimes detach from their surroundings, leading to emotional numbness and difficulty connecting with loved ones.

Psychologically, trauma can manifest as symptoms of PTSD,

including flashbacks and nightmares that bring the traumatic event vividly back to life. Avoidance behaviors may develop, such as steering clear of driving or even being in a car, because these actions trigger intense fear and anxiety. Hypervigilance might also set in, characterized by being constantly on edge, easily startled, and feeling unsafe even in familiar environments. Intrusive thoughts can dominate the mind, with repeated replaying of the traumatic event and constant questioning of what could have been done differently to prevent it.

These manifestations are often triggered by specific events or experiences that unexpectedly connect the present situation to the past trauma. These triggers might be obvious, such as a similar situation, or more subtle, like a particular feeling or even an unrelated event that cues a memory. For instance, a moment of happiness might provoke an unexpected pang of guilt, as the traumatic response suggests that feeling joy is somehow wrong in the aftermath of suffering.

Reflecting on these experiences, it's important to consider whether any patterns or triggers in your life exacerbate your emotional responses to trauma. Identifying these triggers can be a crucial step in understanding and ultimately managing the impact of trauma on your daily life.

Means of Coping

As you navigate the process of healing from trauma, it's important to consider the support systems you currently have or would like to establish. A support system can range from trusted family members and friends to a formal support group, and even extend to hobbies and activities that bring you peace. The presence of these supportive elements can normalize your experience, making the process more manageable and less overwhelming.

A support system forms a crucial part of your coping mechanisms—anything that helps ease the symptoms of trauma. This could include people who listen and offer comfort, as well as activities that calm your mind and restore your sense of balance. Whether it's talking to a friend, engaging in a favorite hobby, or practicing mindfulness, these mechanisms play a key role in helping you manage distress.

Reflecting on what has helped in the past can be valuable. Are there specific coping mechanisms or self-care practices that have provided you relief during difficult times? Understanding what works for you can guide you in building a strong support system and a set of coping strategies tailored to your needs as you continue on your healing journey.

One crucial element of coping with trauma is becoming mindful of how you think and speak about yourself—your inner dialogue or self-talk. The way you engage in this internal conversation can significantly influence your healing process. When reflecting on the trauma, consider how you describe your experiences to yourself. Are you overly critical, perhaps blaming yourself for aspects beyond your control? Do feelings of guilt surface, even though the events were not your fault?

The tone of your self-talk can reveal whether you see yourself as a victim of the trauma or as a survivor who has endured and continues to move forward. Viewing yourself as a victim may suggest that the trauma still weighs heavily on your mind, keeping you trapped in the past. On the other hand, identifying as a survivor can indicate that you are processing the trauma and reclaiming your strength.

Recognizing these patterns in your self-talk is important because they shape your emotional state and influence your ability to heal. Adjusting your inner dialogue to be more compassionate and empowering can help shift your perspective, fostering resilience and aiding in the recovery process.

Your inner strength—whatever form it takes—can be a powerful tool in reframing your traumatic experience and making it less painful to recall. Consider the values or strengths that have helped you navigate challenges in the past. Are you resourceful, resilient, or courageous? These traits can be consciously harnessed to support you in your healing journey, providing a foundation for addressing and processing the trauma.

Reflecting on how these strengths might aid in your recovery can be empowering. For instance, if you've always been resourceful, you might use that trait to seek out helpful resources or coping strategies. If you see yourself as strong and fierce, you could draw on that inner power to face the trauma with determination and courage.

It's important to remember that overcoming trauma is a challenging process, and it's okay to seek help along the way. Professional support, such as therapy, can offer a safe, structured environment in which to explore and process your experiences. A therapist can assist you in renegotiating your narrative, helping you to reframe the trauma in a way that aligns with your strengths and values.

Before engaging in therapy or any form of professional support, it might be helpful to consider what you'd like to focus on. Are there specific aspects of the trauma that you feel ready to confront, or are there areas where you'd prefer to proceed more gradually? Clarifying these points can help you make the most of your sessions, ensuring that the process aligns with your readiness and comfort level.

Envisioning Healing: The Light at the End of the Tunnel

As you journey through the process of trauma recovery, it can be profoundly beneficial to envision how your life and well-being might evolve as you achieve greater ease in processing your experiences. Imagining a future where you feel at peace with your past can serve as a guiding light, illuminating the path forward.

Your psychological transformations begin with the resolution of PTSD symptoms. Envision a state where the relentless grip of flashbacks and nightmares loosens, allowing you to recall the traumatic event without the suffocating fear and anxiety that once accompanied it. This newfound clarity enables you to place the event within the context of your past without it overshadowing your present. You can also enhance your resilience: Imagine yourself imbued with resilience, navigating stress and unexpected challenges with a composed and assured demeanor. Rather than being overwhelmed, you confront life's difficulties with strength and adaptability, fortified by your journey of healing.

Positive cognitive restructuring is another crucial psychological tool: Consider the possibility of reshaping the narrative surrounding your trauma. Instead of viewing it as a defining trauma, you see it as a significant challenge you have overcome, one that has contributed to your growth and deepened your understanding of yourself.

Your physical transformations, on the other hand, may begin with a reduction in your chronic pain. Through the integration of physical therapy, mindfulness practices, and improved mental health, imagine a significant alleviation of chronic pain. Your body responds with greater comfort, and the physical manifestations of stress diminish, leading to enhanced well-being. Improving your sleep quality will also help: Picture yourself enjoying restful, restorative sleep, free from the disturbances of anxiety and pain. You wake each morning feeling rejuvenated, ready to engage with the day ahead with clarity and energy.

Finally, this may lead to an overall health improvement: As you embrace comprehensive self-care practices—including regular physical activity, a balanced diet, and routine health check-ups—your physical health flourishes. You experience a renewed vitality, reflecting the inner healing that has taken place.

Similarly, your emotional transformations begin with emotional balance: Envision experiencing a full spectrum of emotions—joy, sadness, excitement, contentment—without being overshadowed by overwhelming negative feelings. You navigate your emotional landscape with grace and equilibrium, finding harmony within yourself. You may experience renewed connections as well: Imagine rekindling relationships with friends and family, forging deeper and more supportive bonds. The emotional numbness that once distanced you from others dissipates, allowing for meaningful engagement and connection with loved ones. Finally, you'll experience increased confidence: Picture yourself moving through life with a renewed sense of confidence and self-assurance. You feel empowered by your ability to confront and transcend past traumas, carrying this strength into all aspects of your daily life.

Reflecting on these potential outcomes fosters self-awareness and empowerment as you progress through your healing journey. While the process is continuous, the mere act of envisioning a future where trauma no longer holds power over you can begin to reshape your relationship with the past. Engaging in deeper trauma work, particularly with the guidance of a skilled therapist, can facilitate even greater healing, guiding you steadily toward the light at the end of the tunnel.

2

Predisposition Versus Self-Determination

Charlotte hurried down the hallway to her office. An extra half hour at the gym had put her behind for her first appointment. As a clinical psychologist, her tightly packed schedule fueled her sense of accomplishment. It reminded her what she could do when she dedicated herself wholeheartedly. But deep down, Charlotte recognized that her frenetic lifestyle was a deliberate evasion of certain aspects of her life that she wasn't ready to face. Unconsciously, she seemed to believe that by working tirelessly, she could justify excluding everything else from her life.

As she walked through the hallway, she offered polite nods to her colleagues. The pronounced clack of her four-inch Dolce & Gabbana pumps against the marble floor resonated in her ears like music. She adored the idea of those shoes, even though the reality was they made her feet ache dreadfully. Noticing the stark difference between her longing for elegance and the unease it brought, she winced briefly. However, knowing that delving into such deep inner conflicts wasn't appropriate at the moment, she shifted her focus back to work. Settling into her chair, she put on her glasses, wondering what life might be like if she could resist overanalyzing every feeling and sensation. Did life naturally appear simpler to some and more complex to others?

The light on the wall flickered, indicating that Charlotte's first patient had arrived. Charlotte stepped into the waiting room and invited the young woman to come into her office. The young woman scattered her belongings and settled in comfortably. The next hour passed swiftly, as it always did when Charlotte was engaged with a patient. The young graduate student emerged with a mix of relief from processing her thoughts and the lingering disappointment fueled by imposter syndrome.

Looking at the light to check if the next patient was ready, Charlotte cast a final glance around the room to ensure everything was in order. Her eyes fell on a book left behind by the previous patient. This wasn't the first time one of her patients had forgotten something. She retrieved the book and hurried to catch the patient before she left the building. However, as Charlotte reached the elevator, its doors closed, leaving her clutching the book. She wondered if the graduate student would need it before their next appointment and glanced down to discover it was a brand-new Bible.

Upon returning to her office, Charlotte dropped the book into her desk but stared down at the open drawer. She revisited the idea of life's simplicity for some and complexity for others, leading her to engage in a childhood game. She posed a question to the universe, opening a book with the hope that synchronicity would guide her to a verse providing answers.

She thought, *Does life naturally appear simpler to some and more complex to others?* She kept the question in her mind as she randomly chose a page from the Bible. It opened to the story of David and Solomon. Charlotte skimmed the passage briefly until her next patient arrived. Failing to glean much insight from the passage, apart from God granting King David a life of conflict and King Solomon, his son, a life of peace and ease, Charlotte closed the book and proceeded with the rest of her busy day, missing the chance to interpret her findings.

That night, Charlotte found herself lost in thought as she drove home after a grueling ten-hour workday. King David and Solomon played on her mind, igniting a perplexing question: Why do some individuals become the Davids of the world, while others assume the role of Solomons? The notion of God selectively bestowing certain qualities upon individuals left her bewildered. Was it truly the work of a divine force, or could people shape their own lives?

Thinking of the people she had known, she sensed a distinct advantage in the lives of some compared to others. Physical beauty appeared to bestow undeniable blessings upon certain individuals. Some displayed advanced intellectual capabilities that gave them clear advantages. Certain individuals exhibited superior emotional regulation skills. Additionally, circumstances provided inherent advantages, shaping the trajectory of their lives; the place and family of birth profoundly influenced a person's future. Taking all these factors into consideration, how could she dismiss the idea that people were predisposed to certain outcomes in their lives?

Reflecting on the meaning of the word *kismet*, a term deeply ingrained in Eastern culture and signifying destiny, Charlotte found herself entangled between the concepts of predisposition and free will. Since childhood, she had been taught that whatever was destined for her would naturally unfold and what wasn't meant for her would remain out of reach, regardless of her efforts. This notion evoked mixed emotions. On one hand, it offered comfort—an assurance that things would align as intended. On the other hand, it stirred disquiet, as it seemed to absolve individuals of responsibility. This contradicted the fundamental principles of her psychological training, which emphasized accepting personal responsibility and taking action accordingly.

As Charlotte drove home that night, she found herself pondering destiny. If it was preordained at birth, why all the chaos? But if personal willpower truly shaped outcomes, why did it seem some individuals were dealt a better hand in life than others? She saw truth in both perspectives, leaving her bewildered.

Are We Defined by Nature or Our Choices?

In the novel *Memoirs of a Geisha*, the protagonist Sayuri grapples with the conflicting forces of destiny and personal agency.[1]

1 Arthur Golden, *Memoirs of a Geisha* (Alfred A. Knopf, 1997).

Initially, Sayuri feels powerless to influence the course of her life and passively accepts her fate when she is sold to a geisha house as a child. Faced with limited options for women from non-privileged backgrounds, Sayuri believes that becoming a geisha provides a preferable alternative to a life of destitution as a maid or a prostitute. This decision stems from her conviction that she lacks the capability to forge a better future and must submit to her preordained destiny.

Nevertheless, this initial acquiescence to passivity eventually evolves into a quest for freedom and the active pursuit of her own aspirations. Sayuri asserts her identity not as a passive instrument of powerful men but as a woman in control of shaping her own destiny. This transformation underscores the potential of self-determination to reshape one's fate when fueled by a strong enough desire to do so.

Sayuri faces various psychological challenges throughout her life, including her perceived inadequacy of her physical appearance, particularly her gray eyes. In Japanese society during that period, blue-gray eyes were considered less conventionally beautiful. To overcome this psychological barrier, Sayuri learns to use her distinctive features to her advantage rather than viewing them as flaws. Additionally, her journey involves mastering the art of the geisha, which includes cultivating a captivating and enigmatic demeanor, mastering various artistic skills, and refining her social interactions. Through this process, she gains confidence and a sense of self-worth.

Sayuri's psychological resilience and adaptation to societal expectations contribute to her growth and success as a geisha.

The narrative showcases her evolution, demonstrating how she transforms her self-perception in the face of societal norms and personal challenges.

Sayuri's journey underscores the idea that individuals can be active agents in shaping their destiny, even when faced with challenging circumstances or what may be perceived as a disadvantage. Despite the societal norms and the personal struggles she confronts, Sayuri doesn't passively accept her fate but actively works toward transforming her circumstances. Her ability to adapt, learn, and redefine her self-worth highlights the resilience and agency individuals can exhibit in influencing their own destinies, even when dealt a challenging hand. This theme emphasizes the power of personal agency in the face of adversity.

When Life Feels Unfair

One of the most contentious human issues is the concept of fairness. Religious teachings often depict God as merciful, fair, and benevolent. However, from a human perspective, it seems that God does not always deal with people in accordance with what they believe they deserve. According to the scale of justice, those who have endured the greatest hardships should be rewarded the most, and those who have done good deeds should receive life's benevolence. In reality, we often witness the opposite. It appears that, apart from our individual moral compass and the consequences of our actions, there is no definitive evaluation of our deeds in this lifetime.

Individual responses to apparent unfairness are significantly influenced by the person's perceived abilities in relation to their circumstances. Some see themselves as proactive agents armed with the willpower to navigate life's challenges. They approach life with acceptance and, at times, gratitude, making the most of their advantages and working to offset disadvantages within ethical boundaries. Conversely, there are those who feel life has unjustly denied them their due, leading them to adopt one of two approaches. They may surrender to a victim mentality, experiencing a life tainted by bitterness and suffering due to their circumstances. Alternatively, they may embrace a punitive mindset, striving to reclaim what they believe is rightfully theirs, even if it involves resorting to extreme measures that could harm others. They rationalize their actions based on the suffering and pain they have endured.

Regardless of the perceived fairness of life, how we come to view ourselves in this lifetime is heavily influenced by our mindset regarding our individual capabilities. While we may have inherent predispositions that shape our lives, self-determination always offers us the opportunity for optimization through effort, even while acknowledging our limitations. The truth is that no two people have the exact same opportunities in life, because each of us possesses unique abilities and experiences. Often our energy is wasted on comparisons that leave us feeling inadequate and empty. However, through self-reflection, we can tap into our true gifts and potential. Perhaps people are not created equal because they are not meant to live identical lives. Maybe the ultimate goal of this human experience is to truly examine and activate our individual potential according to our own unique path.

Predisposition and self-determination are not opposing modes of relating to life. In fact, viewing them as a spectrum allows us to observe how these two concepts blend and intertwine. By embracing the tension between predisposition and self-determination, we open ourselves up to a potential third option that incorporates elements of both without being limited to either. Our destiny can influence our self-determination, just as our self-determination can shape our destiny.

Igniting Self-Determination and Celebrating Growth

You have the power to change the course of your life. This power lies in actively defining what is important to you and what you truly want, rather than drifting passively through life. When you take the time to clarify your values and goals, you shift from being a mere participant in life to being its architect. This intentional approach empowers you to make decisions that align with your desires and priorities, steering your life in the direction you choose. By actively shaping your path, you assert control over your destiny, ensuring that your actions are purposefully aligned with what matters most to you. In doing so, you transcend the passivity of simply reacting to life's events and instead create a life that is reflective of your true self.

One of the most crucial aspects of living a fulfilling life is ensuring that your actions align with your values and goals. But how can you tell if this alignment exists? The key indicators include consistent satisfaction, emotional resonance, clarity in decision-making, internal harmony, and feedback from others. When your actions are aligned with your values, you typically feel a deep sense of satisfaction and contentment, even when the tasks are challenging; this satisfaction stems from knowing that your efforts are meaningful and true to your core beliefs. Actions that align with your values often evoke positive emotions such as pride, joy, fulfillment; if your actions consistently leave you feeling drained, frustrated, or indifferent, it may be a sign of misalignment.

Alignment also simplifies decision-making; when you know your values and goals, choosing the right path becomes easier, as your decisions naturally reflect what matters most to you. You experience less internal conflict when your actions align with your values. There's a congruence between what you believe and what you do, which reduces feelings of guilt or cognitive dissonance. Sometimes feedback from those around you can provide insight; if trusted friends or mentors comment on how your actions seem to reflect your values and goals, it's a positive sign of alignment.

Aligning your actions with your values and goals is not merely an abstract ideal; it has tangible benefits that significantly enhance the quality of your life. When your actions align with your values, the path forward often feels more straightforward. This alignment creates a sense of purpose that guides you, making the journey less burdensome and more intuitive. Alignment fosters a sense of inner peace and satisfaction, contributing to your overall well-being. Living in harmony with your values reduces stress and anxiety, leading to a healthier, more balanced life.

When your actions reflect your values, motivation is easier to sustain. You're driven not by external pressures but by a deep-seated commitment to your beliefs and goals, which fuels long-term perseverance. Aligned actions provide a strong foundation that helps you navigate challenges. Knowing that you are living in accordance with your values gives you the strength to endure setbacks, as you are anchored by a clear sense of purpose. Ultimately, alignment leads to a life that feels authentic and true. Happiness derived from living in congruence with your values is more profound and lasting than the fleeting satisfaction of pursuing goals that don't resonate with your core beliefs.

To ensure your actions remain aligned with your values and goals, regularly engage in self-reflection. Ask yourself these questions:

- Do my daily actions reflect what I value most?
- Are my goals still aligned with my evolving sense of self?
- Am I making decisions that honor my beliefs and aspirations?

By consistently evaluating and adjusting your actions to stay in alignment, you can create a life that is not only successful but also deeply fulfilling and true to who you are.

Cultivating a Growth Mindset

A growth mindset, a concept popularized by psychologist Carol Dweck, is the belief that abilities and intelligence can be developed through effort, learning, and perseverance. This mindset is crucial because it allows you to view challenges and setbacks not as insurmountable barriers, but as opportunities for growth and learning. Embracing a growth mindset is essential for overcoming obstacles and achieving long-term success.

Obstacles are an inevitable part of any journey, but how you approach them can make all the difference. Begin by understanding the specific challenge you're facing. Is it a lack of resources, a skill deficit, or perhaps an external factor like a difficult work environment? For example, if you're struggling to balance work and personal life, the obstacle might be time management. Approach obstacles with a solution-oriented mindset. Break the problem down into manageable parts and brainstorm possible solutions.

For instance, if time management is the issue, consider strategies like prioritization, delegation, or using time-blocking techniques to create a more structured schedule. Recognize when you need help, and don't hesitate to seek support. This might include asking for advice from mentors, joining a community of like-minded individuals, or utilizing professional resources like coaches or therapists. For example, if you're struggling to develop a new skill, enrolling in a relevant course or finding a mentor could provide the guidance you need. Tap into your internal resources, such as resilience, creativity, and determination. Even if you feel you lack these qualities, they can be developed through practice and self-awareness.

Start by acknowledging your past successes, however small, and build on them. For instance, if you lack confidence in public speaking, start by practicing in smaller, less intimidating settings, gradually increasing the challenge as you improve. Large obstacles can be daunting. Break them down into smaller, more manageable tasks. This approach reduces overwhelm and helps you focus on taking one step at a time. For example, if your goal is to change careers but you feel overwhelmed by the process, start by updating your resume, then move on to networking, and finally begin applying for positions.

A growth mindset is key to turning setbacks into learning opportunities. Cultivate this mindset by first reframing setbacks as learning opportunities: Instead of viewing failures as defeats, see them as valuable lessons. Ask yourself, *What can I learn from this experience?* For instance, if you didn't get a job you applied for, analyze what went wrong—was it a lack of preparation, or perhaps a mismatch in skills? Use this insight to improve your future applications. Welcome challenges as opportunities to grow. When faced with a difficult task, remind yourself that struggling through it is a necessary part of the learning process. For example, if you find coding difficult but essential for your career, embrace the struggle as part of your journey to mastery. When you encounter something you can't do, add "yet" to the end of the statement. For example, "I can't solve this problem" becomes "I can't solve this problem yet."

Small Shifts Make a Difference

This small shift in language reinforces the idea that your abilities can grow with effort and time. Focus on the effort you put into overcoming challenges, rather than just the outcomes. This approach reinforces the value of persistence and resilience, key components of a growth mindset. For instance, if you've been practicing a new skill, celebrate the time and dedication you've invested, regardless of whether you've mastered it yet. Make time to reflect on your experiences, especially after a setback. Consider what you've learned, how you've grown, and how you can apply these lessons moving forward. Regular reflection reinforces a growth mindset by continuously linking effort and learning to personal development.

To enhance your self-determination and effectively overcome obstacles, you need a robust support system and access to valuable resources. Surround yourself with people who encourage your growth and challenge you to reach your potential. This could include mentors, peers, or a community of individuals with similar goals. For example, if you're an entrepreneur, joining a mastermind group can provide the support and accountability needed to overcome business challenges. Find mentors who have navigated similar challenges. Their guidance and experience can provide valuable insights and help you avoid common pitfalls.

What if you want to transition careers? Find a mentor who has made a similar change and can offer advice and support tailored to your situation. Continually seek out opportunities to learn and grow. This might include online courses, workshops, books, or podcasts that align with your goals. If you're struggling with a particular skill, dedicate time to mastering it through these resources. Maintaining your physical and mental well-being is essential for overcoming obstacles. Regular exercise, proper nutrition, sufficient sleep, and mindfulness practices all contribute to a strong foundation that supports resilience and a growth mindset.

Imagine you're aiming for a promotion but were passed over for the opportunity. This feels like a significant setback, leaving you doubting your abilities. You realize that the obstacle might be a gap in specific skills or experience needed for the role. Instead of viewing this as a failure, you reframe it as an opportunity to identify and develop the skills you need to secure the next promotion. You reach out to your supervisor to ask for constructive feedback on why you weren't selected and what areas you should focus on improving. Based on the feedback, you then set specific goals to address these areas—perhaps taking on new projects that stretch your capabilities or enrolling in a relevant course. You remind yourself of past successes and the resilience you've shown in other situations. This boosts your confidence to tackle the new challenges. As you start to see improvement, such as mastering a new skill or receiving positive feedback on your work, you take time to celebrate these milestones, reinforcing your progress. Reflect regularly on your progress, considering what's working and what isn't. This reflection helps you stay on course and make necessary adjustments as you continue pursuing your promotion.

By embracing a growth mindset, seeking support, and strategically addressing challenges, you not only overcome obstacles but also turn setbacks into stepping stones for future success. This approach empowers you to maintain self-determination and resilience on your journey.

Stay Motivated and Focused on Your Goals

Maintaining motivation and focus over time requires strategic action and self-discipline. Begin by defining your goals clearly and ensuring they are specific, measurable, achievable, relevant, and time-bound (SMART). When your goals are well-defined, it's easier to track your progress and maintain focus. Decompose large, overwhelming goals into smaller, more manageable tasks. Each small success provides a sense of accomplishment and keeps you motivated to move forward. Establish a daily or weekly routine that includes dedicated time for working on your goals. Consistency is key; over time, this routine becomes a habit that propels you toward your objectives.

Regularly visualize the successful completion of your goals. This mental rehearsal reinforces your commitment and keeps you emotionally connected to the outcome you desire. Share your goals with a trusted friend, mentor, or coach who can hold you accountable. Regular check-ins provide external motivation and help you stay focused, especially during challenging times. Acknowledge and celebrate even the smallest milestones. Celebrating progress, no matter how modest, keeps motivation high and reinforces the value of your efforts.

Self-reflection and self-awareness are essential tools for personal growth. They help you understand your strengths, recognize areas for improvement, and ensure your actions align with your values and goals. Spend a few minutes each day reflecting on your experiences, emotions, and actions. Journaling helps you track patterns in your behavior, recognize achievements, and identify areas where you can improve. Regular mindfulness practice enhances your awareness of your thoughts and emotions in the present moment. This heightened awareness helps you understand your reactions and make more intentional decisions.

Seek feedback from others who know you well. External perspectives can reveal blind spots and provide valuable insights into your strengths and areas where you might need to grow. Use tools like personality tests, strength finders, or skills inventories to gain a structured understanding of your strengths and areas for growth. These tools complement your self-reflection efforts and provide a more objective view. Set aside time weekly or monthly to evaluate your progress toward your goals. During these sessions, reflect on what's working, what's not, and why. Adjust your strategies as needed to stay aligned with your values and objectives.

Putting New Strategies into Practice

How might these strategies work together in practice? Let's say our example goal is to transition into a new career in finance within six months. You define your goal as obtaining the necessary qualifications and securing an entry-level finance position within six months. You then break this goal into smaller steps: researching finance roles, enrolling in a relevant course, building a network within the industry, and applying for jobs. You establish a routine that includes daily study sessions, weekly networking efforts, and regular job applications. This consistency helps you make steady progress.

Each morning, you spend a few minutes visualizing yourself in a finance role, confidently applying your skills. This visualization keeps you motivated and focused on the end goal. You share your goal with a mentor in the finance industry. Regular check-ins with this mentor keep you accountable and provide valuable guidance along the way. As you complete each course module or secure an informational interview, you take time to celebrate these wins, which fuels your motivation. Weekly, you journal about your progress, reflecting on what you've learned and how you've grown. You also solicit feedback from your mentor and peers, helping you identify areas where you can improve.

Finally, you adjust as needed: During your monthly reflection sessions, you evaluate your progress and adjust your approach. For instance, if a particular networking strategy isn't yielding results, you tweak it based on feedback and self-assessment.

By combining these strategies, you not only stay motivated and focused but also engage in continuous self-reflection and self-awareness. This approach ensures that you remain aligned with your values, adapt to challenges, and steadily progress toward your goals.

Asserting Autonomy and Celebrating Milestones

Asserting your autonomy is about taking deliberate control over your life by making choices that align with your core values and long-term aspirations. Start by deeply understanding your core values and what you aspire to achieve in life. These values act as a compass, guiding your decisions and actions. For example, if you value creativity and aspire to be an artist, ensure that your choices nurture and reflect this passion.

Autonomy is exercised through conscious decision-making. Ask yourself, Does this choice bring me closer to the life I want to lead? For instance, if you're offered a job that doesn't align with your creative aspirations, consider whether it supports your broader goals or if it might lead you away from them. Autonomy also involves setting boundaries that protect your values and time. Learn to say no to opportunities or demands that conflict with your goals. If your value is personal growth, prioritize activities that contribute to that, even if it means declining social invitations that don't serve your long-term aspirations. Taking responsibility for your choices reinforces your autonomy. Recognize that every decision, whether it leads to success or a setback, is a step on your journey. This mindset empowers you to learn from experiences and continuously align your actions with your values.

Celebrating your achievements, both big and small, is essential for reinforcing your sense of self-determination and accomplishment. Don't wait for major milestones to celebrate. Recognize and celebrate small wins along the way. For example, if your goal is to write a book, celebrate each chapter you complete. These small celebrations keep you motivated and reinforce your progress. Link your celebrations to rewards that resonate with your values. If you value experiences, treat yourself to a day trip or an event that enriches your life. For instance, after completing a major project at work that aligns with your career aspirations, reward yourself with a weekend getaway that allows you to recharge and reflect.

Keep on Planning Next Steps

Take time to reflect on what each achievement means to you. Journaling about how far you've come and the effort it took to get there can deepen your sense of accomplishment. This reflection helps you internalize your success and appreciate the growth that has occurred.

Sharing your milestones with loved ones can amplify your sense of achievement. Whether it's through a celebratory dinner, a small gathering, or even a simple conversation, sharing your success not only reinforces your accomplishment but also strengthens your support network. After celebrating a milestone, take time to plan your next steps. This practice ensures that your celebrations fuel future progress rather than becoming a stopping point. For example, after celebrating a successful presentation, set new goals for further professional development.

Let's say you've decided to pursue a career in photography, a field that aligns with your value of creativity and your aspiration to express yourself through visual art. You recognize that creativity, freedom, and self-expression are your core values. You decide that your career path should allow you to explore these fully. When offered a high-paying corporate job that doesn't align with your creative aspirations, you choose to decline. Instead, you take on freelance photography projects that, while less lucrative, allow you to build your portfolio and develop your unique style.

You set boundaries around your time, dedicating weekends and evenings to personal photography projects, even if it means declining social activities that don't align with your creative goals. You fully commit to your choice, acknowledging that the freelance path may be challenging but is ultimately more fulfilling. You own the outcome, whether success or setbacks, as part of your journey.

After booking your first paid photography gig, you celebrate by purchasing a new lens, a tool that further supports your creative work. Upon completing a significant photo series, you reward yourself with a solo retreat to a location that inspires your creativity, allowing you to recharge and reflect on your journey. You keep a journal where you document your growth, noting how each project has helped you refine your skills and solidify your style. This reflection reinforces your sense of accomplishment and autonomy. You share your completed photo series with close friends and family, celebrating with a small gallery event. Their support and appreciation amplify your sense of achievement. After celebrating the successful series, you set new goals, such as submitting your work to photography contests or starting a new, more ambitious project. This ensures that your growth continues.

In this example, asserting autonomy and celebrating milestones are intertwined in a way that continuously reinforces your values, aspirations, and sense of self-determination. Each choice and celebration fuels your journey, helping you build a life that is authentically yours.

Self-determination and empowerment are cultivated through key practices such as introspection, goal-setting, resilience, and proactive decision-making. Introspection involves examining one's thoughts and beliefs, providing the self-awareness necessary to make decisions aligned with personal values rather than external influences. Goal-setting then translates this self-awareness into actionable objectives, structuring efforts toward personal and professional aspirations, and reinforcing a sense of agency.

Resilience, the ability to recover from setbacks, ensures that challenges are met with adaptability and growth rather than hindrance, supporting continuous progress. Proactive decision-making further enhances empowerment by enabling individuals to make deliberate choices that reflect their long-term goals, fostering a life of intention where decisions are aligned with personal impact and purpose.

The benefits of integrating these practices are significant: greater autonomy in life decisions, enhanced self-esteem from achieving goals, improved mental well-being through better stress management and reduced anxiety, and ultimately a deeper sense of fulfillment by living a life aligned with one's true values. Through these elements, individuals cultivate a resilient and empowered self, laying the foundation for a fulfilling, purpose-driven life.

3

Physical Versus Emotional Pain

That night, Charlotte took a long bath. She immersed herself in the soothing scent of lavender bath salts while listening to Tchaikovsky's Symphony No. 2 and sipping a glass of wine. Leaning her head against a rolled-up towel to support her neck, she let her mind begin to wander, but her peace was abruptly interrupted by the doorbell.

Dragging herself out of the tub, Charlotte wrapped herself in a robe. Leaving wet footprints on the floor, she approached the front door and unlatched it without asking who was on the other side.

As she swung the door open, she froze. Standing in the hallway was Adam, the love of her life and the perpetrator of her most painful betrayal. The last time she saw him was three years ago, but she remembered the details of their last night together as if they'd been etched into her brain—a snapshot of emotion. Adam had been wearing a dark suit with a crisp white shirt, complemented by her favorite cufflinks, engraved with his initials. The two of them walked hand in hand down 3rd Street after sharing an amazing dinner at her favorite restaurant. That night, with a full moon in the sky, the city had never appeared more enchanting. She allowed the bliss of love to shine through her like the moonlight. She still remembered the innocence with which she admired him. In her world, he was a king put there just for her to worship.

But he crushed that feeling when he cheated on her.

As Charlotte gazed into the eyes of the man standing at her doorstep, she searched for the love of her life, but all she could see was a man who had disappointed her. Over the years, she had convinced herself that it was merely infatuation; otherwise, he wouldn't have done what he did. She didn't want to acknowledge the extent of the pain he had caused her. But in moments of weakness, she could admit that she still truly cared for him, even though it hurt. Admitting she cared for him would mean she was weak—or worse, that she had allowed him to play her. The alternative was to imagine he didn't matter that much to her—and somehow, that thought felt more tolerable. So she changed her inner dialogue to that narrative, even though those who knew her well understood exactly what Adam meant to her and how much she had been destroyed by his actions.

Now, with him standing at her doorstep, the years of unspoken resentment and unresolved pain hung between them like a thick, suffocating fog. The longing look in his eyes hinted at his intentions—perhaps an apology or even an attempt to mend what was broken. But Charlotte's heart, hardened by years of bitterness, couldn't see past the disappointment and betrayal. She hesitated, torn between the part of her that still ached for closure and the part that wanted to protect herself from further hurt.

After a brief, tense silence, she stepped back slightly, leaving the door ajar—a small gesture that could have been an invitation, although she wasn't sure why she'd done it. Deep down, she knew she wanted to hear what he had to say, but the fear of being hurt again was too overwhelming to allow her to be vulnerable.

Adam hesitated, seeming to have lost his confidence. Finally, he managed a tentative "Hello."

Charlotte could see he was struggling, but instead of softening, her frustration only grew. It was as if the sight of him—this man who had once meant everything to her—was too much to bear. She didn't want to give him the satisfaction of knowing how deeply he had affected her, how much she still cared. Her voice, sharp and tinged with bitterness, cut through the silence. "Are you lost?"

Her sarcastic tone, intended to shield her vulnerability, only served to inflame the tension. The longing expression on his face quickly turned to anger, his eyes narrowing as he took a step back. "You know, I despise your arrogance. It's what kept me away all this time," he shot back, his voice rising with frustration.

In that moment, the toxicity of their interaction became painfully clear. Instead of confronting her true feelings, Charlotte had lashed out, pushing him away before he could hurt her again, and he reacted in anger at her rejection. She knew that whatever he had come here for—reconciliation, forgiveness—it was off the table now. The cycle was familiar, a toxic dance they had repeated many times before—miscommunication, hurt, and anger feeding off each other until the chance for real connection was lost. The truth was, she didn't know how to navigate the raw emotions that lingered between them, and she suspected that he didn't either. They were both too proud, too wounded, to be the first to extend a genuine olive branch.

Something snapped in Charlotte at that moment. The hurt and the unresolved emotions boiled over, and before she could think it through, she slammed the door shut with a resounding thud. As she leaned against the closed door, her breath coming in ragged gasps, she whispered to herself, "Then you should have stayed away."

Her hands were trembling, and she felt rage and fear and sadness all at once. How had he managed to evoke such intense emotions in her within a matter of seconds? Her near-perfect peace of moments before had been shattered. She loathed the power he held over her and despised herself for allowing him to wield it. Charlotte had believed she'd dealt with these emotions and moved on, but now they resurfaced with a vengeance, overwhelming her once again. Lightheaded, she stumbled into the kitchen, desperately reaching for a glass of water. She gulped it down so hastily that she almost choked, her hand still shaking.

She sank to the floor, seeking solace in the battle between her heart and her mind. The emotional part of her yearned to rush back to the door, to run into his arms and pretend that the painful past had never happened. She longed to express how much she missed him, to feel close to him again. However, a wise inner voice kept her grounded, reminding her of the pain she had endured—that he had caused. With agonizing acceptance, she whispered to herself, "You're going to be okay. Just breathe."

It took a long time before she found the strength to rise and walk back to her bedroom. Defeated and hopeless, she questioned whether love was meant to be so excruciating. Nothing in the world seemed worth this overwhelming grief, especially after all this time. She glanced at her phone to see whether he had texted—secretly hoping he had; but the blank screen dashed her short-lived fantasy. She wondered why he had shown up at her apartment, and she chastised herself for her initial openness and for her sarcasm. She wished she had remained calm and invited him in, but deep down, she knew better. The emotions were too raw, too complex for her to maintain composure.

Underneath the comforting embrace of white satin sheets, she closed her eyes, desperately hoping that this painful encounter would fade into a distant memory by morning.

Why Does Emotional Pain Hurt More than Physical Pain?

The brain mechanisms responsible for physical pain are also linked to emotional distress. The human body addresses pain through a dual mechanism involving both physical injuries and negative emotional reactions. While it's more straightforward to grasp this association when dealing with a physical injury, where both blood and the injury site substantiate the pain, emotional pain is more elusive. In emotional distress, there's no visible blood or physical injury to rationalize the pain. Nevertheless, the emotional turmoil evokes a similar sense of discomfort and, in some instances, even more intense feelings for the individual.

The deep-rooted connection instinct in humans predisposes us to experience negative emotions when confronted with separation from a loved one or any other psychological distress. How we perceive this pain is a blend of numerous complex dynamics in the physical body and psyche. Emotional pain isn't just a mental experience; it's deeply physical, affecting how our bodies function in tangible ways. Picture it like a symphony of responses.

First, neurotransmitters like serotonin, dopamine, and norepinephrine start playing their part. When emotions hit, these chemicals shift, influencing whether we feel positive or negative emotions. Then, the hormonal stage lights up. Our hypothalamic–pituitary–adrenal axis springs into action, releasing cortisol and adrenaline, the stress hormones. Imagine them as the conductor, orchestrating our body's response to emotional distress. Next, the autonomic nervous system takes center stage. It has two key players: the sympathetic nervous system, triggering our fight-or-flight mode with increased heart rate and heightened arousal and activating the parasympathetic nervous system to bring calm and relaxation after the storm. Our brain's backstage crew—the amygdala, prefrontal cortex, and anterior cingulate cortex—work tirelessly. They process emotions, make decisions, and even interpret pain signals, shaping how we experience and react to emotional pain. Meanwhile, the endocrine system adds depth to the performance. Oxytocin fosters bonding and connection, while endorphins act as natural pain relievers, softening the emotional blows. Last, the immune system joins in, responding to chronic stress and emotional distress. Like background dancers, they showcase how emotional pain can weaken our defenses, leaving us vulnerable to health issues. Understanding this symphony of physical responses not only brings clarity to emotional pain but also guides us toward effective strategies for managing it and nurturing our overall well-being.

The human body often reacts to emotional distress with a fight-or-flight response, treating perceived pain as an external threat. Whether confronting physical dangers or emotional challenges, the body prepares for action by directing blood flow to the muscles. Consequently, digestion slows down, resulting in a feeling of queasiness. Initially, emotional pain may emerge as an unpleasant memory. However, due to its emotional intensity and the need for further processing, the memory replays persistently, evolving into a distinct and recognizable mood.

Individuals undergoing emotional pain often characterize themselves as being in a negative mood due to their identification with the experienced emotions. As the script of the traumatic event is revisited multiple times, the negative mood persists and, if not properly addressed, evolves into a more enduring state known as temperament. Unprocessed traumatic events can, in the long term, adversely impact an individual's emotional well-being by influencing their self-perception, their perceptions of others, and their view of the world. Conversely, proper processing can lead to a correction of these negative associations.

Remaining in this prolonged physiological and psychological state can lead an individual to perceive themselves as victims of circumstances. The victim mentality, which can be deeply debilitating, carries the danger of ensnaring someone in a negative mindset indefinitely. Those with this mindset often believe they lack the power to change their situation, falling into a pattern of learned helplessness that may manifest as extreme passivity or passive-aggressiveness. This is fundamentally a restrictive mindset; there is always a path for action when dissatisfaction arises. Consider Thomas Edison's journey of facing failure ten thousand times before inventing the light bulb—an illustration of refusing to be victimized by outcomes and persisting in seeing oneself as an active participant in shaping life's course.

For this transformation to occur, the physiological response to that trauma has to be shifted. The degree of emotional pain we experience is not solely dictated by the actual traumatic event. Once the initial shock diminishes, what perpetuates emotional pain is our interpretation of the event and the perceived sense of control over the subsequent events. Those who see themselves as capable agents in control of their lives may effectively reauthor the remaining chapters of their story with greater ease and optimism. For this to happen, the physiological response to that trauma has to be shifted.

Reclaiming Agency and Cultivating Self-Compassion

Disidentifying from psychological pain is a powerful way to regain a sense of agency and control over emotional experiences. This process involves recognizing the source of discomfort, understanding the thoughts and beliefs that contribute to it, and then detaching from those thoughts to see them as separate from one's identity.

Consider a situation where someone consistently feels inadequate at work. The thought *I'm not good enough* becomes a recurring narrative, leading to emotional distress. This thought might be triggered by external events, such as receiving criticism or comparing oneself to others.

Identifying with this thought can serve a subconscious purpose. For instance, believing you're not good enough might protect against the fear of failure. By accepting this narrative, there's an excuse to avoid taking risks or striving for more, thereby avoiding the potential pain of disappointment. In this way, identifying with the pain becomes a kind of comfort zone, shielding from deeper fears or challenges.

Disidentifying from psychological pain means recognizing that the thought *I'm not good enough* is just that—a thought, not a defining truth. This process involves questioning the validity of the belief: Is this thought actually true? What evidence exists to contradict it? By disidentifying from the pain, the person can see that their worth isn't determined by a single thought or feeling. This realization allows them to view the situation more objectively, reducing the emotional intensity tied to the belief.

Disidentifying from psychological pain brings several key benefits: Realizing that feelings of inadequacy are not the ultimate truth allows for a regained sense of control over one's life. There's an understanding that it's possible to change the narrative and, as a result, change the emotional experience. Seeing pain as a transient state rather than an intrinsic part of identity reduces the intensity of emotional suffering. The pain can be acknowledged without allowing it to dominate. Disidentification empowers the person to make positive changes. They can start setting goals, seeking feedback, and improving skills without being held back by limiting beliefs. Disidentification also opens up the mind to alternative viewpoints. Compliments, constructive criticism, and new opportunities are received with a more balanced and less defensive mindset.

Imagine someone receives a critical performance review at work. The initial thought might be *I'm not good enough*, leading to a familiar sense of inadequacy. Instead of fully identifying with this thought, the person pauses and acknowledges it as just a thought. By questioning the thought—Is this really true? What are other possible interpretations of this feedback?—the person disidentifies from the pain and gains a more objective perspective.

The performance review is then seen not as a judgment of worth but as an opportunity for growth. This shift allows for proactive steps, such as seeking additional training or mentoring, which in turn boosts confidence and competence. Over time, with continued practice of disidentification, the belief that they're not good enough loses its power. The person becomes more resilient, and setbacks are viewed as learning opportunities rather than as confirmations of inadequacy.

Disidentifying from psychological pain is a crucial step in regaining control over emotional experiences. By recognizing thoughts and emotions as separate from identity, emotional suffering can be reduced and a sense of agency can be restored. This process not only alleviates pain but also fosters personal growth and resilience.

Observing Thoughts and Emotions: Achieving Helpful Detachment

Observing your thoughts and emotions without getting entangled in them is a powerful skill that fosters emotional resilience and self-awareness. This detachment allows you to acknowledge your pain without being overwhelmed by it. However, if you find it challenging to achieve this level of detachment, there are strategies you can employ to cultivate it.

If you struggle to observe your thoughts and emotions without getting caught up in them, to develop this skill, start with mindfulness exercises, which focus on bringing attention to the present moment without judgment. Through regular mindfulness practice, you can learn to notice your thoughts and emotions as they arise, acknowledging them without immediately reacting or becoming immersed in them. This creates a mental space between you and your thoughts, making it easier to observe rather than engage.

Another technique is to label your thoughts and emotions as they come up. For example, when you notice a thought like *I'm not good enough*, you might say to yourself, *I'm having the thought that I'm not good enough*. This subtle shift in language reinforces the idea that your thoughts are not facts but simply mental events passing through your mind.

Visualize your thoughts as leaves floating down a stream or clouds passing by in the sky. This imagery can help you see thoughts and emotions as transient, rather than something you need to hold on to or engage with. This technique encourages a sense of detachment, making it easier to observe without getting caught up. Engage in deep breathing exercises to calm your nervous system. When you're feeling overwhelmed by your emotions, taking slow, deep breaths can help you step back and regain a sense of control. Focusing on your breath anchors you in the present moment and can reduce the intensity of emotional responses.

Achieving this level of detachment offers several benefits: Detachment helps you respond to situations with greater clarity and calmness, rather than reacting impulsively based on heightened emotions. This leads to better decision-making and a more balanced emotional life. Observing your thoughts and emotions from a detached perspective enhances self-awareness. You become more attuned to the patterns of your thinking and the triggers for your emotions, which allows you to address them more effectively. Detachment also empowers you by reinforcing the idea that you are not defined by your thoughts or emotions. It strengthens your sense of agency, as you realize that you can choose how to respond to your inner experiences rather than being controlled by them. Over time, practicing detachment builds emotional resilience. You become less susceptible to being overwhelmed by negative emotions and more capable of handling stress and adversity with composure.

Earlier, we discussed the idea of recontextualizing painful memories to reduce their emotional impact. By learning to observe your thoughts and emotions without getting caught up in them, you are, in essence, recontextualizing your present experiences. Just as you reframe memories to alter their influence over you, you can detach from current thoughts and emotions to prevent them from dictating your mood and actions.

Imagine you're facing a challenging situation at work, and the thought *I'm going to fail* keeps surfacing. Instead of immediately panicking or letting the thought spiral into more anxiety, you take a deep breath and mentally label the thought: *I'm having the thought that I'm going to fail.* You visualize this thought as a leaf floating down a stream, acknowledging its presence but letting it pass by without clinging to it.

By practicing this level of detachment, you reduce the emotional charge of the thought. You're able to approach the situation with a clearer mind, making it easier to focus on potential solutions rather than being paralyzed by fear. Over time, as you continue to observe and detach from your thoughts, you build the capacity to face challenges with greater calm and confidence.

The ability to observe your thoughts and emotions without getting caught up in them is a key step in regaining control over your emotional life. If this skill doesn't come naturally, it can be developed through mindfulness, labeling, imagery, and breathing techniques. This detachment not only reduces emotional reactivity but also enhances self-awareness, empowerment, and resilience—tools that are essential for navigating both present challenges and recontextualizing past experiences.

Cultivating Self-Compassion and Understanding amid Psychological Pain

Self-compassion is the practice of being kind and understanding toward yourself, especially during difficult times. It's about treating yourself with the same care and empathy you would offer to a friend in need. Cultivating self-compassion is crucial for healing because it helps break the cycle of self-criticism that often exacerbates psychological pain. When you approach your pain with compassion, you create a safe space within yourself to process emotions, which can lead to greater resilience and emotional well-being.

When you're experiencing psychological pain, it's common to blame yourself or feel inadequate. Self-compassion counteracts this by encouraging you to treat yourself gently and without judgment, which reduces the intensity of negative emotions. By being compassionate with yourself, you build emotional resilience. This means you're better able to cope with setbacks and challenges because you're not adding self-inflicted emotional wounds on top of the pain you're already experiencing. Self-compassion provides the emotional support needed to heal. It allows you to acknowledge your pain without becoming overwhelmed by it, facilitating a more balanced and constructive approach to recovery.

Asking whether there are underlying fears or insecurities amplifying your experience of pain is crucial because these elements often lie at the root of psychological suffering. For example, if you're struggling with feelings of rejection, there may be an underlying fear of abandonment or a belief that you're unworthy of love. These fears and insecurities can intensify your pain and make it harder to move forward.

Reflect on what specific fears or insecurities might be contributing to your pain. For instance, if you're feeling anxious about a relationship, consider whether this anxiety stems from past experiences of rejection or fear of not being good enough. Once you've identified these fears, challenge them. Ask yourself, *Is this belief true? What evidence do I have that contradicts it?* This process helps you weaken the hold these fears have over you. Sometimes, addressing deep-seated fears and insecurities requires external support. Speaking with a therapist, counselor, or trusted friend can provide new perspectives and coping strategies.

Acceptance is a key component in disidentifying from psychological pain. It involves acknowledging the presence of pain without trying to suppress or deny it. Acceptance doesn't mean resignation; rather, it's about recognizing that pain is a part of your current experience without letting it define you.

To practice acceptance, start by acknowledging that the pain exists. Instead of pushing it away or pretending it's not there, allow yourself to fully experience it. This might mean sitting with uncomfortable emotions or admitting difficult truths to yourself. Resistance to pain often intensifies it. By practicing acceptance, you let go of the struggle against your emotions. This doesn't mean you like or want the pain; it simply means you recognize it as part of your experience in this moment. Mindfulness can help you practice acceptance by keeping you grounded in the present moment. When painful thoughts or feelings arise, observe them without judgment and let them pass without getting caught up in them.

Seeing your pain as a temporary experience rather than a permanent aspect of your identity is crucial for healing. This reframing allows you to understand that pain is just one part of your life, not the entirety of who you are. Remind yourself that your pain is an experience, not a reflection of your worth or character. For example, instead of saying *I am a failure*, reframe it as *I am experiencing failure in this situation, but it doesn't define who I am*. Remind yourself that pain is often temporary. While it may feel overwhelming now, it won't last forever. This perspective can help you endure difficult moments with the knowledge that they will eventually pass. Sometimes, reframing pain involves finding meaning in the experience. Ask yourself, *What can I learn from this? How can this experience contribute to my growth?* This approach can help you see pain as a stepping stone rather than a stumbling block.

Strategies for Managing Psychological Pain and Cultivating Self-Compassion

For those who find themselves caught in the cycle of psychological pain, the journey toward regaining a sense of control begins with cultivating distance from the distress. This detachment can be achieved through various practices that calm the mind and offer new perspectives.

Box breathing is a method where one inhales, holds the breath, exhales, and holds again, each for a count of four. This simple practice can interrupt the cycle of emotional overwhelm, bringing a sense of calm and clarity. By focusing on the present moment, mindfulness meditation encourages a gentle observation of thoughts and emotions without judgment, fostering a sense of detachment from the pain. Shifting one's perspective on a distressing thought or situation can alter its emotional impact. Viewing setbacks as opportunities for growth rather than as failures can reduce their hold on one's psyche. Engaging in movement, whether through a brisk walk or more deliberate exercise, can serve as a powerful tool to shift focus and release pent-up emotions, grounding the mind in the present.

Moments of clarity and peace, even in the midst of psychological turmoil, often arise from certain activities that resonate on a deeper level. These practices can provide a respite and a window into more sustained relief. Articulating thoughts and feelings on paper can bring clarity, helping to untangle complex emotions and reveal underlying patterns. Activities like painting or music offer an outlet for emotions that may be difficult to express verbally, providing relief and a sense of accomplishment. The simplicity of being in nature, whether through walking or simply observing, can have a grounding effect, quieting the mind and offering a broader perspective.

Support systems and resources are crucial in the process of disidentifying from psychological pain—recognizing that pain does not define one's identity but is a transient experience. Engaging with a therapist can provide a structured environment for exploring painful thoughts and emotions, offering tools for disidentification and healing. Regular engagement with mindfulness can help solidify the practice of observing thoughts without becoming entangled in them, reinforcing the notion that pain is a passing experience. Connecting with others who share similar experiences can reduce feelings of isolation and offer practical advice, helping one to see that their pain is part of a shared human experience rather than a defining characteristic.

Acceptance is a subtle yet profound practice in managing psychological pain. It involves acknowledging the presence of pain without letting it dominate one's identity. Reframing this pain as a temporary state rather than a permanent trait allows for a more resilient and empowered approach to life. Viewing pain as a temporary experience that offers opportunities for growth can diminish its power. This shift in perspective allows for a more balanced emotional response and fosters resilience.

In essence, by cultivating self-compassion and practicing acceptance, one can create the necessary distance from psychological pain, leading to a more empowered and resilient way of being. Disidentifying from pain, through these practices and resources, allows for a clearer perspective and a deeper understanding of the transient nature of suffering.

The Importance of Underlying Beliefs and Self-Compassion in Managing Psychological Pain

The questions posed encourage a deeper level of introspection and self-awareness, crucial for uncovering the underlying beliefs that often drive psychological pain. These beliefs, whether consciously acknowledged or not, shape how individuals perceive and respond to their experiences. By identifying and evaluating these beliefs, one can begin to understand the root causes of their distress and take steps toward healthier, more constructive ways of thinking.

Underlying beliefs are the silent architects of our emotional world. They inform how we interpret events, how we perceive ourselves, and how we interact with others. For example, a belief that you're not worthy can lead to feelings of inadequacy, anxiety, and depression, influencing everything from career choices to relationships. By bringing these beliefs to light, individuals can challenge and reframe them, replacing destructive patterns with more empowering ones.

The goal of identifying and addressing these beliefs is to shift from a reactive state—where one is at the mercy of these internalized narratives—to a proactive state, where one can consciously choose how to respond to life's challenges. This transformation leads to greater emotional resilience, improved mental health, and a stronger sense of agency.

Self-compassion plays a pivotal role in this process. It involves treating oneself with kindness and understanding during times of pain or failure, rather than succumbing to self-criticism. The benefits of cultivating self-compassion are profound: Self-compassion helps individuals bounce back more quickly from setbacks. By offering themselves the same kindness they would offer a friend, individuals can reduce the impact of negative emotions and prevent downward spirals into self-blame.

Those who practice self-compassion are less likely to suffer from anxiety and depression. They are better equipped to handle stress and are less likely to engage in harmful self-criticism. Self-compassion fosters a sense of acceptance, helping individuals embrace their imperfections without harsh judgment. This acceptance is crucial for maintaining a positive self-image and nurturing personal growth. By being compassionate toward themselves, individuals are more likely to extend the same kindness and understanding to others. This leads to healthier, more empathetic relationships.

The ultimate goal of engaging in this process of introspection, identifying underlying beliefs, and cultivating self-compassion is to achieve a state of empowerment and emotional resilience.

As individuals become more aware of the beliefs that drive their behavior, they gain the ability to challenge and change them. By practicing self-compassion, they build the emotional strength needed to navigate life's challenges with grace and confidence.

In this end state, psychological pain no longer dominates one's identity. Instead, it becomes a manageable aspect of life, approached with understanding and handled with care. This transformation leads to a more balanced, fulfilling life, where individuals are not only better equipped to manage their own emotions but also more capable of fostering positive relationships and achieving personal goals.

4

Innocence Versus Experience

When Charlotte opened her eyes in the morning, the weight of her memories pressed down on her like a heavy blanket. The battle within her mind had left her body weary, and the scars of past hurts made it difficult to rise and face the day. The memory of a line from a long-forgotten documentary about snakes resurfaced: "Nobody actually dies from a snakebite; it's the venom that kills." Charlotte felt the venom of her emotional wounds coursing through her veins, poisoning her thoughts and clouding her heart. She yearned to release it, to reclaim her emotional freedom, but the path to healing was not as straightforward as she had hoped.

She had been trying to move forward, to let go of the resentment that clung to her like a second skin—the hurt she felt after he betrayed her. This morning, however, the old wounds felt raw, and the progress she thought she had made seemed distant. In an attempt to find solace, Charlotte closed her eyes and embarked on a visualization exercise. She imagined a space free from negative thoughts, emotions, and sensations, but the dark tendrils of doubt and regret kept creeping in. It was a struggle, a battle between the desire for peace and the reality of her pain.

As she went about her day, Charlotte couldn't shake the feeling of emptiness that lingered beneath the surface. She had missed her usual workout, a sign that she was not as in control as she liked to believe. Rather than fretting over it, she tried to focus on self-care, but even the thought of pampering herself felt hollow. With a lighter load of patients, she decided to visit her favorite spa later in the evening, hoping the familiar routine might offer some comfort. Yet, the anticipation of an afternoon of relaxation was tinged with unease. Could she really escape the weight of her thoughts, even for a few hours?

That morning, while waiting in line at the bakery on her way to work, Charlotte struck up a conversation with a woman named Elli who stood ahead of her. As they talked and Elli learned that Charlotte was a psychologist, she felt compelled to open up about her doubts regarding the choices she had made in life, questioning whether her entire life had been wrong. Recognizing Elli's need for support, Charlotte offered her a business card, extending a compassionate offer to listen and provide potential referrals. Elli graciously accepted, promising to reach out when she needed someone to talk to.

This encounter brought to Charlotte's mind a poignant line from Leo Tolstoy's novel *The Death of Ivan Ilyich*, where the protagonist, Ivan Ilyich, is haunted by the question, "What if my entire life has been wrong?"[2] Elli's words echoed this very sentiment, prompting Charlotte to reflect deeply on her own life. She couldn't help but consider her own regrets and the opportunities she feared had slipped away, as Ivan's question now resonated within her as well.

As the day wore on, thoughts of Adam began to intrude. He had reappeared in her life unexpectedly, showing up at her doorstep after three years of silence. The memories of their time together flooded back. He had been a symphony of culture, ambition, kindness, and passion. But he had also hurt her deeply. The duality of her feelings toward him left her conflicted. Had she been naive to believe in the perfection she once saw in him? Was she now wise enough to see him as just another flawed human being, or was she still clinging to an idealized version of him?

She wondered how he had found her; she had refused to take his calls or see him after the breakup, and she had taken every precaution to safeguard her address due to the confidentiality she needed with her job. There was a time when she had viewed Adam as the epitome of everything she desired. He had been the kind of man who seemed to understand her in ways no one else ever had. But that was before he turned against her, before she

2 Leo Tolstoy, *The Death of Ivan Ilyich* (The Russian Messenger, 1886).

saw the darker sides of him that contradicted the perfect image she'd created in her mind.

In her earlier years, Charlotte had been innocent in her belief that love could be simple, that Adam's faults were minor blemishes on an otherwise flawless surface. She had ignored the subtle signs—the possessiveness disguised as protectiveness, the charm that masked manipulation, the passion that too often veered into obsession. She had been blinded by the allure of what she thought they could be together.

But now, years later, with the benefit of experience and the scars to prove it, Charlotte could see the truth. Adam was not the idealized figure she had once believed him to be. He was a flawed, confused man—just like anyone else. The duality between the man she had once loved and the man who had hurt her was now stark in her mind. The question that gnawed at her was whether she had truly come to terms with that reality. Was she now experienced enough to recognize that her initial innocence had clouded her judgment? Or was she still clinging to the false belief that she had fully healed, that she could now judge her emotional well-being with clear eyes?

The truth was, Charlotte wasn't sure. Some part of her still feared the man who had once been her everything. But was she afraid of Adam, or was she afraid of what he represented—a reminder of her own vulnerability, her own capacity for self-deception?

As she reflected on their breakup, the memories flooded back with painful clarity. It wasn't just the end of a relationship; it was the shattering of an illusion. The night in New York had been the breaking point. Adam's words had cut deep, revealing a side of him she had refused to see. His accusations, his anger, his refusal to let her go peacefully—they had all left lasting wounds. And yet, even now, she found herself questioning whether she had made the right choice, whether she had missed out on something that could have been salvaged.

This was the duality she struggled with—the tension between her innocence and her experience, between the idealized love she had once believed in and the harsh reality of what that love had become. Charlotte realized that she wasn't as healed as she had convinced herself she was. The process of letting go, of truly moving on, was far from over. Adam's reappearance had reopened old wounds, forcing her to confront the parts of herself that were still entangled in the past.

Charlotte couldn't help but wonder if Adam represented a story of unfulfilled potential in her life. What if she had stayed with him that night in New York? What if things had been different? The questions gnawed at her, and she found herself spiraling into a sea of what-ifs. The realization that she had taken precautions to safeguard her address only deepened her unease. Why had he looked for her now? What did he want?

Later, during her massage, Charlotte tried to clear her mind, but the tension in her body mirrored the turmoil in her thoughts. The soothing lavender oil did little to calm her racing mind. Regret—something she tried to avoid—was seeping in, and she wasn't sure how to confront it. She had always prided herself on making the best choices she could with the information she had at the time. But was she lying to herself? Was there a part of her that regretted leaving Adam, or even being with him in the first place?

Charlotte realized that she had been telling herself she was healed, that she had moved on. But now, in the quiet of the massage room, she had to face the truth: Healing wasn't a straight line, and she was still on the journey. The past wasn't as distant as she wanted to believe, and the venom of her emotional wounds hadn't fully dissipated. As she breathed in the calming fragrance, she knew she had more work to do—more reflection, more acceptance, and perhaps, more forgiveness.

The Loss of Innocence Through Experience

Innocence is commonly associated with youth, and its loss is often accompanied by a sense of darkness and vulnerability. The notion of losing your innocence can be interpreted in various ways, and depending on the perspective, it may occur multiple times throughout your life. Innocence can also represent the purity of believing in the best outcomes from people and circumstances. This natural inclination is prevalent among those who have not yet been exposed to the harsh realities of life. However, once experiences of treachery have been imprinted on our mind, it becomes challenging to return to that state of innocence. Conversely, it is all too easy to become entrapped in the darkness of life, falling into pessimism or cynicism. Those who face early hardships often struggle to maintain their innocence and may unintentionally cross into the realm of justified immorality. The true challenge lies in accepting the responsibilities of life without sacrificing your morality.

Certain cultures and tribes have rituals that initiate young adults into the loss of innocence, guiding them toward the realm of adulthood. These practices aim to expose them to life's complexities, teaching coping skills and better preparing them for the challenges ahead. The idea of innocence is often specific to a person's culture or religion, centering on something that society deems sacred.

Cultural rituals like bar mitzvahs and quinceañeras not only symbolize the loss of innocence and the transition to adulthood but also hold psychological significance. These rituals involve psychological shifts, shaping identity and responsibilities. The Japanese Coming of Age Day—*Seijin no Hi*—at the age of twenty and initiation ceremonies in various African cultures are similar. They guide members of the community from childhood innocence into the complexities of adulthood, influencing psychological development within cultural contexts. This transition signifies the acquisition of knowledge, responsibility, and a heightened awareness of the complexities of the adult world. It serves as a bridge connecting the simplicity of childhood to the nuanced challenges of adulthood. Shedding innocence is essential for each of us to navigate life's intricacies, contribute meaningfully to our communities, and embark on a journey of personal growth and self-discovery. This transformative process allows us to fully engage with the world, equipped with the tools needed for a fulfilling and purposeful life.

Nonetheless, there are various paths to losing innocence, and every individual undergoes this transformation at least once in their life. If the loss is not processed properly, it can lead to emotional distress. When confronted with the harsh and potentially brutal realities of life, we undergo an adjustment period where we adopt a new worldview. For instance, a child who unexpectedly loses a parent is suddenly confronted with the reality that the world is not always a safe place and that unfortunate events can occur at any moment. While this realization holds some truth, internalizing it as a mantra can be detrimental to the child's emotional well-being, because it portrays an overly pessimistic worldview. An alternative perspective is recognizing that this reality is just one aspect of life and that safety and positive experiences also exist. The question then arises: How do we continue to believe in the good after repeatedly facing the bad?

The loss of innocence can lead to a negative worldview, leaving you feeling victimized and powerless in the face of life's challenges, or it can serve as a catalyst for emotional growth, enabling acceptance of life's realities from a position of strength. Adopting either mindset is a personal choice that we each have the power to make. Each time we encounter a difficult situation, we are presented with an opportunity to find ways to navigate through it, inviting self-expansion and personal growth. If we learn to respond to these invitations with resilience and adaptability, we continue to develop our sense of self. However, if we allow ourselves to be defeated by these attempts, bitterness and resentment may take hold.

The loss of innocence is an inevitable part of life. Regardless of how blessed we may be, we repeatedly face defeats in this lifetime. However, rather than finding this reality demoralizing, we can view it as an opportunity to exchange our naive belief systems for more seasoned ones, ultimately fostering personal growth and wisdom.

Rebuilding and Gaining Wisdom After Innocence Is Lost

The loss of innocence can be a profound and challenging experience, often requiring deep introspection and self-awareness. This process may involve revisiting moments in life where your beliefs, values, or worldview were fundamentally altered by a particular event or series of events. Start by reflecting on a time when you felt a significant loss of innocence. What specific event triggered this change? It's important to recognize that this isn't necessarily a singular moment; many people experience a loss of innocence multiple times throughout their lives.

Consider the experience of discovering that a trusted friend has betrayed your confidence. This revelation may lead to a profound sense of loss, altering your trust in others and changing the way you perceive relationships. The emotions surrounding such a loss can be complex, involving feelings of anger, sadness, and confusion.

After identifying the event that led to your loss of innocence, reflect on how it has affected you. Did it shift your beliefs and values? What emotions did you experience at the time, and how do you feel about it now? Often, these experiences can lead to a reevaluation of previously held assumptions, pushing you to reconsider what you believed to be true about yourself, others, or the world at large. Following a betrayal, you might find yourself more guarded in relationships, questioning the trustworthiness of others. This shift in perspective might be accompanied by a sense of loss, not just of the relationship, but of the naive belief that others could be implicitly trusted.

Rebuilding trust and a sense of security after such a loss is a critical part of the healing process. This can be particularly challenging, as the foundation of your previous beliefs has been shaken. To begin this process, consider who you can turn to for support. This might include close friends, family members, or a therapist who can offer guidance and understanding as you navigate these feelings. You might choose to confide in a friend or seek professional help from a therapist who can provide a safe space to explore your feelings of betrayal and help you rebuild your sense of trust. Therapy, in particular, can offer structured support, helping you to process the loss and develop strategies for moving forward.

As you work through the emotions tied to the loss of innocence, it's important to reevaluate your values and beliefs. Consider which aspects of your previous worldview you want to retain and which ones you might let go of. This process allows you to adapt your beliefs to align more closely with your current understanding and experiences. After a difficult experience, you might decide that while it's important to be cautious, it's also essential not to lose the capacity for trust altogether. You may choose to approach new relationships with a more discerning eye, but without the cynicism that can close you off from meaningful connections.

Transforming a loss of innocence into an opportunity for personal growth is a powerful way to move forward. Ask yourself how this experience has shaped you and how you can use it to become stronger, more resilient, and more self-aware. The betrayal might lead you to set clearer boundaries in relationships, ensuring that you communicate your needs and expectations more effectively. This could strengthen your future relationships and empower you to maintain a sense of agency and self-respect.

Moving forward requires actionable steps toward healing. These might include engaging in self-care practices, seeking out new experiences that restore your sense of trust and security, or continuing to work with a therapist to process lingering emotions. You might start by journaling about your feelings, practicing mindfulness to stay grounded in the present, or gradually opening yourself up to new social situations where you can practice trust in a controlled, safe environment.

Finally, consider what innocence means to you now. After going through the healing process, innocence may no longer represent naivety, but rather a sense of openness and trust tempered by experience. This redefined innocence can be a source of strength, allowing you to engage with the world through wisdom and compassion, rather than fear or disillusionment. Innocence might come to symbolize a balanced perspective—one that acknowledges the potential for harm, but also recognizes the possibility of goodness and growth in every new experience.

These questions and reflections serve as starting points for exploring the complexities of dealing with the loss of innocence. By approaching this process with self-compassion and patience, you can navigate your healing journey, allowing for the time and space needed for growth and transformation. Through introspection, support, and intentional action, you can emerge from this experience with a deeper understanding of yourself and the world, and with a renewed sense of strength and resilience.

While the loss of innocence often feels like a moment of disillusionment, it also marks the beginning of a new phase of self-discovery. This part focuses on the active process of rebuilding and reorienting yourself after such a loss. Begin by acknowledging that this experience, though painful, has fundamentally altered your perspective. This acknowledgment is not just about understanding the event but about accepting the impact it has had on you. Consider the experience of realizing that a long-held belief—such as the idea that hard work always leads to success—is not as straightforward as you once thought. This realization might occur after facing repeated setbacks despite your best efforts. Acknowledging this loss means coming to terms with the complexity of the world and recognizing that life is influenced by many factors beyond your control.

After experiencing a significant loss of innocence, it's common to feel a sense of identity shift. This chapter encourages you to actively reconstruct your identity in a way that integrates your new understanding of the world. This involves reassessing who you are now, in light of what you've learned, and consciously choosing how you want to move forward. If the belief in guaranteed success through hard work has been challenged, you might begin to see yourself not just as a hard worker but as someone who is adaptable, resilient, and capable of finding value in the journey, not just the destination. This reconstructed identity is richer and more nuanced, reflecting the depth of your experiences.

Embracing Complexity

The loss of innocence often comes with the realization that the world is not as black-and-white as it once seemed. Embracing this complexity is a crucial step in the rebuilding process. This chapter guides you to accept that life is filled with contradictions and uncertainties, and that embracing these complexities can lead to a more mature and grounded perspective. Rather than viewing setbacks as failures, you might start to see them as opportunities to develop resilience and problem-solving skills. Embracing complexity means understanding that success isn't linear and that growth often comes from navigating challenges rather than avoiding them.

As you rebuild, you may find that your previous values no longer fully resonate with your new understanding of the world. This chapter encourages you to cultivate new values that align with your evolved perspective. These values might be more flexible, adaptable, and grounded in the reality of your experiences. For example, after losing the belief that success is guaranteed by effort alone, you might place more value on perseverance, learning, and adaptability. These new values reflect a deeper understanding of what it means to grow and succeed in a complex world.

Unlike the initial belief system described above, the new mindset can strengthen your resilience in the face of future challenges. This involves developing coping strategies, seeking out supportive relationships, and engaging in practices that foster emotional and mental strength. You might begin to practice mindfulness or engage in regular physical activity as a way to build resilience. Additionally, surrounding yourself with supportive individuals who share or respect your new values can help reinforce your growth and provide a strong network to lean on during difficult times.

Here success is reexamined and redefined. Where once success might have been seen in terms of external achievements, it is now understood as a more internal, personal sense of fulfillment. This shift reflects the deeper, more nuanced understanding of life that comes after the loss of innocence. Success might now be defined by your ability to maintain integrity, to continue learning, and to adapt to changing circumstances with grace and resilience. Fulfillment becomes less about achieving specific outcomes and more about living in alignment with your evolved values and identity.

This process is not just about healing from the loss, but about consciously choosing how to move forward with a deeper, more nuanced understanding of yourself and the world. By reconstructing your identity, embracing complexity, cultivating new values, building resilience, and redefining success, you lay the foundation for a life that is both richer and more resilient, equipped to navigate the challenges that come with maturity. This marks a turning point where the focus shifts from recovery to proactive growth, ensuring that the lessons learned from the loss of innocence lead to a more empowered and fulfilling life.

5

Journey Versus Destination

When Charlotte got home, she picked up her phone and thumbed through her contacts to Kara. Her sister's voice on the other end gave her hope that she might find some answers to ease her inner turmoil. The sisters danced around some small talk and chatted about their upcoming vacation together. When Charlotte's tension reached a peak, she casually asked, "Have you heard from Adam lately?" She heard a nervousness in her own voice that only those who knew her well could detect.

"Adam who?" her sister asked. Kara had never been subtle in her matchmaking attempts, and her feeble attempt to hide the truth only confirmed Charlotte's suspicion.

Politely, Charlotte asked, "Kara, I'm not mad at you, but can you just tell me the truth?"

Kara apologetically murmured, "I ran into him at Annabel's a couple of weeks ago. He was in London for business, and he spent the entire night following me, hoping to get information about you. I didn't mean to upset you. Please don't be mad."

A silence hung between them for a moment, heavy with the weight of Kara's admission. Charlotte felt a mix of confusion and anger. Should she be upset with Kara for engaging with Adam behind her back, or was there a part of her that was secretly pleased that Adam still cared enough to ask about her? But the more she thought about it, the more the anger simmered.

"Kara, I really wish you hadn't talked to him about me," Charlotte finally said, her voice steadier than she felt. "You know how hard I've been trying to move on, and hearing this just—it brings everything back."

There was a pause on the other end of the line before Kara spoke, her tone laced with regret. "I'm really sorry, Charlotte. I didn't think it would hurt you like this. I just thought that, maybe, it would help to know that he still cares."

Charlotte sighed, feeling a mixture of frustration and sadness. "I get that you were trying to help, but it wasn't your place to decide what's good for me. If you had told me earlier, maybe I could have prepared myself. But now it just feels like you kept something important from me. It complicates everything."

After a long moment, Kara's voice came through, soft and full of apology. "You're right. I should have told you. I never wanted to hurt you."

Charlotte closed her eyes, trying to push down the emotions that were bubbling up. She wasn't sure how she felt. Was she angry at Kara for reopening this old wound, or was she secretly pleased that Adam still cared enough to inquire about her? Charlotte wished she had outgrown the situation enough to simply be angry, without the tangle of mixed emotions. But deep down, her inner wisdom reminded her that emotions don't always work that way. She finished the call and reflected on the love she once felt for him. She thought about the journey of love lost versus the destination of a perfect love story ending. Perhaps not all stories were meant to have a happy ending.

She began reminiscing about her journey with Adam, which had started at a Christmas Eve celebration. Charlotte had always loved Christmas, believing it to be a truly magical time when anything could happen. That particular night, captivated by the twinkling lights and the enchantment of the season, Charlotte was having dinner with her mother. As was often the case, Charlotte felt a sense of unease under her mother's critical gaze, leading her to drink more than she normally would. When she excused herself to visit the restroom, she stumbled slightly in her heels. For a moment, she considered taking them off, but the disapproving look she anticipated from her mother deterred her. After all, the last thing she needed was to give her mother another reason to be disappointed.

She cautiously ascended the stairs but suddenly lost her balance and tumbled. Terrified of the impending fall, she closed her eyes, preparing for the impact. However, before she could hit the ground, a pair of strong hands caught her, keeping her upright. Grateful, she clung to this stranger, but she was too afraid to open her eyes, and she trembled slightly in his arms. In response, he drew her closer. After a few seconds, she mustered the courage to open her eyes and gaze up at the stranger who had caught her. It was a tall, handsome man—Adam.

Her story with Adam had begun with a chance encounter on that fateful Christmas Eve. He had playfully called her the best Christmas gift he had ever received, and she couldn't help but feel the same way. Meeting a handsome stranger who had saved her from a fall down the staircase only reinforced her belief in the magic of Christmas and its power to bring about unexpected connection. Despite the serendipity of their meeting, Charlotte consciously decided to see where the relationship could lead, drawn to Adam's charm and the way he made her feel. She chose to invest in the relationship, believing that sometimes the most meaningful connections begin unexpectedly, but grow through intentional choice and commitment.

Thinking back, Charlotte wondered whether she had imbued their story with more meaning than it truly held, especially the way it had ended. Perhaps she wanted it to be more than it was—a forever fairy tale. Despite the intense emotions they shared, a part of her inner wisdom knew that nothing in this world was meant to last forever. Maybe all she was meant to experience with Adam was a fleeting love. Maybe their story wasn't destined for a happy ending, and perhaps that was okay.

Charlotte's thoughts turned to the human tendency to simplify and justify situations. In her work as a psychologist, she had witnessed people trying to find meaning in their hardships, attempting to justify why they had to endure certain challenges.

Some schools of thought believed that creating meaning could help humans process difficulties with greater ease. Yet deep down she understood that not everything in life could be neatly explained or justified. Sometimes things simply happened, and no amount of searching for meaning could make sense of it.

The truth was that Charlotte had shared a brief, magical love story with Adam. Everything that came afterward—the reality of a normal relationship—fell short, and the painful ending left her with a profound ache that defied justification. She knew the only way to navigate this pain was to allow herself to feel it, bit by bit, in the hopes that one day it would hurt less. Strangely, she found solace in accepting that Adam's part of her story was just that—a part of her larger story, separate from what she had wanted it to be. It was time to acknowledge that his part of her story had run its course.

Charlotte resolved to embrace the lessons she had learned from this beautiful and painful part of her journey and move forward. The magic of Christmas would still hold a special place in her heart, but she understood that not every story had to follow a conventional narrative. Sometimes, the most significant growth came from accepting the chapters that didn't end as expected.

Is the End More Important Than the Path?

In Western culture, life is frequently interpreted from binary perspectives—success or failure, winners or losers. The emphasis is heavily on attaining an endpoint, and we often neglect the inherent value of the journey. From our youth, narratives teach us to pursue perfection, to excel in every endeavor. Those who have accomplished remarkable feats often emphasize the significance of the journey in shaping their most memorable experiences. Yet when we miss our objectives, we often diminish the journey as futile, convinced that without achieving the destination, our efforts were unrewarding.

Ironically, promises shape the narratives of our lives. In our formative years, parental guidance echoes, "Success in life demands the sacrifice of youth for a better tomorrow. Study diligently now, and a brighter future awaits." As we navigate the challenges of midlife, juggling career responsibilities and family obligations, the refrain changes: "Diligence in one's prime leads to the rewards of later years." Each life stage conditions us to trade the present moment for an envisioned tomorrow. Yet what if tomorrow eludes us? Perhaps it's time to shift our perspective, cherishing the journey rather than fixating solely on the destination. This way, even if our intended goals remain unrealized, we would have embraced the true essence of life.

In recent years, the mindfulness trend has placed a significant emphasis on the importance of the present moment, aiming to redirect focus from a future-dominant mindset. However, various misinterpretations surround this concept. Many perceive staying in the present as a license to defy norms and pursue immediate satisfaction, irrespective of consequences. Mindfulness, in essence, advocates for honoring the moment just as we cherish the past and future, urging us to consciously choose our actions by understanding the inherent value of the present.

The journey embodies change, transformation, and the revelation of our latent potential. It pulses with the vitality of life, radiating the energy of continual evolution. It serves as our muse, propelling and motivating us, enabling access to our inner reservoirs of strength. Conversely, the destination marks the culmination of the quest—a point where the ultimate goal is achieved. In the destination, the energy settles, because the striving has reached its conclusion.

Moreover, the destination often comes with conditions that may breed disappointment. Upon reaching a goal, we might realize the satisfaction is transient, fueling a desire for the next endeavor. Alternatively, the achieved goal may prove less fulfilling than expected, resulting in a sense of despair. The journey, in contrast, is unconditional. Regardless of the outcome, the experience remains an integral part of us. By appreciating the intrinsic value of the journey, we can find joy in the process without attaching conditional expectations.

The journey encourages joy without attachment, because it allows us to appreciate things for what they are, free from rigid definitions. In contrast, the destination promotes attachment, tying our appreciation to the fulfillment of specific desires and outcomes. While there is undeniably value in reaching a destination, acknowledging that every journey leads to a point of arrival, the emphasis on the journey lies in the joy found along the way, independent of fixed outcomes.

Both the journey and the destination are valuable, yet life predominantly consists of the journey. Placing sole emphasis on the destination deprives us of fully relishing the diverse experiences woven into the fabric of life. Emotional pain often stems from an overemphasis on the destination at the expense of the journey, fostering false hopes that may remain unattainable. Artfully embracing each aspect for its unique offerings and comprehending the intrinsic purpose of both represents a skill that will enable you to embrace joy more holistically in your life.

Balancing the Journey with the Destination

In the pursuit of personal growth, career advancement, or life goals, it's common to focus heavily on the destination—the end result we're striving for. However, the journey, with all its lessons, challenges, and experiences, is equally important. Striking a balance between the two is key to a fulfilling and meaningful life.

To begin, reflect on the specific goals or outcomes you are aiming for in your life, career, or personal development. These are your destinations. For example, you might be working toward a promotion at work, completing a degree, achieving financial independence, or cultivating deeper relationships. Each of these is a tangible goal that signifies a specific outcome. If your goal is to achieve a promotion, your destination might be defined by the new role, the responsibilities it entails, and the recognition it brings. For someone focused on personal development, a destination might be becoming more confident or achieving a particular level of expertise.

Next, consider how you define success or achievement in these areas. Is success reaching a certain milestone, such as earning a specific salary, finishing a project, or attaining a certain level of expertise? Identifying these milestones helps clarify what your destination looks like. For the goal of a promotion, milestones might include completing certain projects, gaining new skills, or receiving positive feedback from supervisors. In personal development, milestones might be recognizing growth in confidence through handling difficult situations with more ease.

Aspects of the Journey

While it's important to have clear goals, focusing solely on the destination can lead to missing out on the richness of the journey. The journey is where growth happens—through the challenges faced, the setbacks overcome, and the learning that takes place along the way. Ask yourself what aspects of the journey toward your goals you find most fulfilling or meaningful. For example, do you value the learning that occurs as you tackle new challenges? Do you appreciate the relationships you build and the insights you gain along the way? In the pursuit of a promotion, you might find fulfillment in the new skills you acquire, the collaboration with colleagues, and the sense of achievement that comes from overcoming obstacles.

Consider how you approach challenges, setbacks, and unexpected detours. Are you resilient and adaptable, viewing these moments as opportunities for growth? Or do you see them as obstacles that delay your progress? Your approach to these experiences reveals your focus on the journey. A person who views setbacks as learning opportunities may feel a sense of satisfaction from the journey itself, recognizing that each challenge makes them stronger and more prepared for future success.

Achieving a balance between focusing on the destination and appreciating the journey involves taking a step back to reflect on your experiences and acknowledging the value they bring. It's about recognizing that while goals are important, the path to reaching them offers valuable lessons and growth opportunities.

If you find yourself overly focused on outcomes, you might miss out on the present moment and the small, significant achievements that happen daily. Balancing your focus allows you to enjoy the process, which can enhance your motivation and well-being.

A balanced approach helps you stay grounded and present, reducing stress and preventing burnout. It allows you to appreciate your progress and the learning that happens along the way, making the entire experience more meaningful and fulfilling. When you balance your focus, you not only reach your goals but also grow as a person, developing resilience, adaptability, and a deeper understanding of yourself and your values.

To strike this balance, make it a habit to regularly reflect on your progress and the lessons you've learned. Take time to appreciate the relationships, experiences, and personal growth that occur as you work toward your goals. You can take actionable steps such as daily reflection. Spend a few minutes each day reflecting on what you've learned and how you've grown. Acknowledge and celebrate the small milestones and successes along the way. And keep a journal to record moments of gratitude related to your journey—whether it's a new skill learned, a helpful conversation, or a challenge overcome.

By balancing your focus between the destination and the journey, you gain clarity on your priorities and motivations, ensuring that you approach both aspects in a meaningful way. This balance leads to a more fulfilling life, where you're not just chasing goals but enjoying the process of growth and discovery along the way.

Balancing the journey with the destination provides a sense of purpose and fulfillment that extends beyond simply achieving a goal. It enriches your experience, helps you stay motivated, and fosters a deep sense of contentment with your life's path.

6

Connection Versus Disconnection

Charlotte had diligently attended therapy sessions every ten days for the past decade. Each session unfurled fresh layers of her psyche, enthralling her with its complexities and inspiring further introspection. However, on this particular day, she departed her therapy session feeling more confounded than ever. She had opted to confront an internal dichotomy, a conflict that had lingered for many years. Despite earnest attempts to reconcile these two parts of herself, she acknowledged that the more she grappled, the more elusive resolution became. She longed to reconnect with Adam, but she also dreaded seeing him again. She was overwhelmingly curious about his perspective, but was also dedicated to remaining resolute in her convictions. Through all the emotions, there was a part of her that wanted to stay away and another part that was still very drawn to him.

Conflict raged within Charlotte—a struggle between the vulnerable, emotional part of her that yearned to comprehend Adam's intentions and the logical, resolute part that recognized she possessed all the essential information. No clear victor emerged in this conflict, and Charlotte often found herself on the losing side.

With her eyes closed, Charlotte sat in her car as a solitary tear traced down her cheek. Once again, she craved clarity and wished for someone to offer answers. She had mentioned it during her therapy session, and she continued to process and struggle. She knew this was a crucial part of therapy, no matter how difficult it was in the moment. For the umpteenth time that day, she compelled herself to reconcile these conflicting forces, seeking integration. Lost in thought, she began to drive, oblivious to the passing car beside her. The persistent honking from the other driver snapped her back to the present but also triggered thoughts of her past.

Memories of the accident site hijacked her mind, overwhelming her with vivid recollections. In books, she had read about how people who lost one sense would rely on their remaining senses, perceiving the world through a different lens. Although she couldn't see immediately after the accident, she possessed enough awareness to navigate her surroundings using her sense of hearing. Amid the chaos, her mother's voice asking questions acted as a familiar melody to Charlotte's ears, assuring her that her mother was still alive. Despite the repetitive nature of her mother's questioning, a result of trauma-induced delirium, Charlotte found patience within herself. She calmly responded to her mother's inquiries time and time again.

The blaring siren of the ambulance drowned out her mother's voice, and Charlotte attempted to rely on her sense of touch to determine her surroundings. She felt herself being moved and realized she was being placed on a gurney. The voices around her were numerous, issuing instructions to one another. From their conversations, she deduced that her injuries were severe. The medics hurriedly attended to her, their frantic touches moving from one body part to the next as they tended to her wounds. She didn't recall feeling any physical pain, but the commotion unsettled her.

Charlotte yearned for the chaos to stop. In an attempt to gather as much information as possible, she focused her remaining senses. As the paramedics exchanged instructions for the next steps of her treatment, she felt vulnerable and helpless, desperate to cry out, but she couldn't find her voice. Summoning every ounce of energy, she reached out her hand and tightly grasped the hand of one of the paramedics. Longing for human connection and seeking solace in the touch she solicited, she held on.

Even in that chaotic moment, Charlotte instinctively understood the importance of human connection. Her training in trauma response reminded her of the significance of staying connected to others during times of distress as a means to avoid dissociation. She recognized that dissociation often served as a self-protective survival technique, allowing individuals to escape overwhelming physical and mental states. However, she also knew that maintaining a connection to the environment through positive experiences was crucial in preventing this primitive coping mechanism. Charlotte was aware that succumbing to dissociation would carry emotional repercussions, potentially leaving a part of her trapped in that state even if she physically survived. In her attempt to minimize emotional damage, she regulated her nervous system and avoided further harm.

The paramedic removed Charlotte's hand from his arm as he continued his work. She could hear their conversation about the injury to her head and left eye, discussing the need to locate and halt the source of bleeding before reaching the hospital. Each word heightened her fear. Uncertain about the greater distress—the talk about her state without any explanation to her or about the gravity of her lacerations—she grappled with fear while remaining physiologically numb.

She felt a needle pierce her arm, and a sense of calm began to settle. The voices around her faded, and it felt as if she were being drawn into a haze. She attempted to resist the sensation, a part of her desiring to stay alert and have some say in the process. But there was also a seductive allure to the idea of sleeping through this ordeal. Eventually, she yielded, allowing the medication to take over.

Behind Charlotte's car, another blaring horn startled her, snapping her back to the present, where she'd been holding up traffic at a green light. Offering an apologetic wave, she cautiously began to drive, her legs trembling slightly. In that moment, she wondered whether her healing experience would have been different had she been in a more supportive environment during the accident.

Human connection during a traumatic event significantly impacts the psyche by influencing how the brain processes and responds to the trauma. From a scientific perspective, the presence of social support can activate the attachment system, which provides a sense of safety and security. This connection triggers the release of oxytocin, a hormone associated with bonding, which can dampen the brain's stress response by reducing the activity of the amygdala, the area responsible for fear and anxiety. Additionally, when people share their experiences with others, it facilitates cognitive processing of the traumatic event, helping to integrate it into their life narrative and preventing the development of distorted beliefs often associated with trauma, such as self-blame. The validation and reality testing provided by social connections help in accurately assessing the reality of the event, thereby reducing the likelihood of maladaptive thoughts and emotions that could lead to conditions like post-traumatic stress disorder. Overall, human connection serves as a crucial buffer against the long-term psychological effects of trauma, promoting resilience and recovery.

The rest of her drive home was anything but pleasant as she continued to struggle with her emotions about Adam while wrestling with the ghosts of her past. Recognizing a link between these struggles, she realized the necessity of letting go of both Adam and the accident. Despite her desire to continue processing everything, she was mentally and physically drained. All she could do was to put a pin in it, allowing herself to set it aside for now until she had the inner capacity to revisit and address it all. She knew that when you go through something like this, no matter how many people you are surrounded by, the experience feels very lonely. She'd have to process this by herself no matter what.

Why Is It Hard to Build Lasting Connections?

As humans, our natural desire for meaningful relationships extends to our interactions with others and our inner selves. The deepest joy and fulfillment often arise from moments of closeness, prompting us to pursue chances to expand these encounters. By participating in activities that ignite our enthusiasm or sharing moments with those we cherish, we can cultivate a profound sense of satisfaction by fostering genuine bonds.

Connection to ourselves and others is paramount in the journey of personal growth and fulfillment. Understanding yourself—embracing your emotions, thoughts, and values—forms the cornerstone of self-connection, fostering inner harmony and self-awareness. Through practices of self-compassion and mindfulness, we can deepen our relationship with ourselves, nurturing a sense of acceptance and resilience.

Equally vital are relationships with others, where empathy, active listening, and vulnerability are the threads that weave bonds of trust and understanding. Sharing experiences, thoughts, and emotions with loved ones nurtures a sense of belonging and support, strengthening the fabric of community and social connection. In this interplay between self-discovery and interpersonal relationships lies the essence of human experience—a delicate dance of introspection and connection, shaping our journey toward wholeness and meaning.

Physical touch is one of the most common and impactful ways of fostering connection. It transcends verbal communication, offering a direct and tangible form of expressing emotions, comfort, and support. Whether through a warm hug, a reassuring handshake, or a gentle touch, physical contact holds the power to deepen bonds and create a profound sense of closeness between people. This primal form of connection satisfies our innate need for physical proximity and understanding, contributing significantly to the richness of meaningful relationships, be it in friendships or romantic partnerships.

Touch is a powerful avenue for experiencing connection. It has been linked to feelings of association and relatedness. When we are touched by another person, we develop a sense of connection in that moment. Physical touch activates the vagus nerve, which interfaces with the parasympathetic nervous system, leading to a decrease in heart rate, blood pressure, and stress hormone levels. Additionally, touch stimulates the release of oxytocin, a natural painkiller, and enhances the immune system. In infancy, human touch is crucial for the production of oxytocin and vasopressin, which play a significant role in social bonding. This impact of touch continues throughout our developmental years.

A controversial study conducted in 1940 demonstrated the vital role of touch in human development. Two groups of infants were raised in a sterile environment and attended to with the necessary care, but one group received regular physical touch while the other had limited touch. After four months, half of the infants in the touch-deprived group had died due to a lack of affection and touch.

Despite its importance, nonsexual interpersonal touch is less common in individualistic cultures. The concept of touch has been surrounded by controversy, especially in relation to potential sexual harassment allegations.

Touch can also be a profoundly delicate subject for individuals with a history of abuse, as it can evoke traumatic memories, trigger intense emotional reactions, and exacerbate feelings of vulnerability and a loss of control. Survivors of abuse often struggle to trust others and may feel uncomfortable or threatened by physical contact, even if it's intended to be supportive. The violation of personal boundaries during abuse can make it challenging for survivors to differentiate between healthy and unhealthy forms of touch, leaving them with mixed messages and confusion. Reclaiming agency over their bodies and setting clear boundaries around physical touch are essential aspects of the healing journey for these individuals, who navigate a complex process of healing and self-discovery. It's crucial for others to respect their boundaries and offer support in ways that feel safe and empowering, recognizing that healing from past abuse is a deeply personal and ongoing journey.

To add another level of complexity, in the wake of the 2020 pandemic, fears of viral transmission have further complicated people's attitudes toward touch. Moreover, individualistic cultures often have different rules and boundaries when it comes to personal space, allowing for less physical intimacy between individuals.

It's essential to recognize that while touch is a prevalent means of connection, connection itself is not limited to physical touch alone. There exist myriad avenues through which individuals can forge connections. These avenues encompass various forms of communication, expression, and interaction, each unique to the individual. From verbal communication and shared experiences to acts of kindness and empathy, connection transcends the boundaries of touch. It encompasses the bonds formed through shared laughter, deep conversations, mutual understanding, and heartfelt gestures.

Connection Means Interaction

Whether through shared interests, emotional support, or simply being present for one another, the essence of connection lies in the genuine and meaningful interactions that enrich our lives and nurture our relationships. While touch may signify one aspect of connection, it is but one thread that weaves through the fabric of our existence.

Despite our innate inclination toward connection, it's a common human experience to encounter pain stemming from connectedness. This pain can arise from various sources such as abandonment, loss, or relationship breakdowns. In response, we often instinctively resort to protective defense mechanisms, such as disconnecting. This serves as a means to safeguard ourselves from further hurt. However, while these defenses offer a sense of safety, they can also impede genuine connection and intimacy. When individuals associate connection with past hurts or traumas, the instinctual survival mechanism of disconnection may be triggered.

In understanding disconnection, we delve into the intricate workings of the human nervous system, where both the sympathetic and parasympathetic branches play pivotal roles. The sympathetic nervous system, known for its fight-or-flight response, often comes into play when individuals perceive threats or stressors. In such instances, disconnection may emerge as a protective mechanism, shielding individuals from perceived danger or emotional distress. However, disconnection also finds its roots in the parasympathetic nervous system, particularly in the freeze response. As the body enters a state of immobilization in the face of extreme fear or threat, a sense of numbness or emotional shutdown may ensue—a form of disconnection from the surroundings or emotions. The dance between the sympathetic and parasympathetic nervous systems unfolds, shaping our responses to the challenges and stressors encountered in life's journey. Since the parasympathetic nervous system controls vital functions such as digestion, sleep, immune functioning, and circulation, any disruption in its functioning can lead to significant dysfunction, resulting in feelings of confusion, numbness, and disconnection. Without appropriate therapeutic intervention to guide the individual out of this state, they may remain trapped in a prolonged state of dysfunction.

During a traumatic event, dissociation serves as a coping mechanism to endure the pain of the moment, but it can also disrupt the functioning of the nervous system going forward. The ability to connect with others emotionally and physically can significantly impact the level of dissociation experienced during and after trauma. Regardless of the traumatic experience, the path to healing involves reestablishing connections that are not associated with pain or harm for the individual.

Dissociation is the experience of becoming ensnared in the ceaseless tumult of the mind rather than dwelling in the visceral realm of bodily sensations. It transpires when enduring the present moment becomes an arduous and overwhelming endeavor. A vast majority of us instinctively resort to dissociation as a means of enduring the status quo. Remarkably, the more undesirable the circumstances, the more profound the dissociative state tends to become.

This phenomenon invites contemplation and exploration, delving into the intricate interplay between our thoughts and physical experiences. Understanding how we navigate this delicate balance can offer insight into our coping mechanisms, resilience, and our ability to embrace or disengage from the world around us.

Engaging the five senses can be a highly effective way to shift from dissociation back into a state of connection and presence. When we intentionally focus on our sensory experiences, we ground ourselves in the present moment and reconnect with our physical bodies and the environment around us. This practice can be particularly valuable for individuals who experience dissociation as a coping mechanism during challenging or overwhelming situations.

This technique is a powerful way to deepen our connection with the present moment and cultivate a heightened sense of mindfulness. When we deliberately pay attention to what we see, hear, taste, smell, and touch, we anchor ourselves in the richness of our immediate experience. This sensory awareness not only brings us closer to the world around us but also fosters a profound connection with our own bodies. It's a practice that invites us to savor the intricate tapestry of life's sensations, promoting a greater sense of presence, gratitude, and inner peace in an often fast-paced and distracted world.

Strengthening Bonds Through Vulnerability

Fostering connection begins with a profound internal journey, where self-connection forms the bedrock of meaningful relationships with others. The process starts with understanding the fundamental beliefs and principles that have shaped your identity and guided your life choices. These core values are the compass of your life, influencing your decisions and interactions with the world around you. Reflecting on these beliefs, perhaps by writing them down, can illuminate how they have shaped who you are and how they guide your actions. This introspection is crucial as it leads to a deeper sense of self-awareness—an ongoing exploration of your emotions, thoughts, and motivations. Through this process, you learn not only who you are but also how to navigate your life with greater intention and clarity.

Self-compassion and self-forgiveness play a vital role in this journey. These practices are essential because they allow you to embrace your imperfections, fostering inner growth and resilience. By treating yourself with kindness, you create an environment where healing and transformation can occur, which is necessary for cultivating a strong and resilient connection with yourself. Incorporating self-care rituals into your daily routine, such as meditation, exercise, or journaling, strengthens this connection and builds your capacity for handling life's challenges. These rituals not only provide comfort but also reinforce your mental and emotional well-being, ensuring you remain balanced and grounded.

In your relationships with others, qualities like trust, empathy, and authenticity are crucial. These qualities are not only reflective of the kind of relationships you seek but also of the kind of person you strive to be. If you find that these qualities are not aligned with the people around you, it may indicate a need to reevaluate those relationships or to set clearer boundaries. Boundaries are essential because they protect your well-being and help maintain healthy, respectful dynamics. For instance, establishing boundaries around your time and emotional energy ensures that your relationships remain balanced and fulfilling.

Expressing gratitude and appreciation for the unique contributions of those you care about is another key to deepening connections. Gratitude is powerful; it reinforces positive interactions and fosters a supportive environment, making your relationships stronger and more resilient. Mutual understanding, achieved by approaching conflicts or disagreements with curiosity and a willingness to understand different perspectives, is fundamental to sustaining harmony in relationships. This understanding not only helps resolve conflicts but also deepens the bond between individuals, ensuring that relationships are resilient and enriching. Communication strategies such as active listening, using "I" statements, and avoiding judgmental language are effective in ensuring that your interactions are clear, compassionate, and nonjudgmental. By cultivating these practices, you not only foster meaningful connections but also contribute to creating a more empathetic and compassionate world.

7

Comfort Versus Discomfort

Charlotte stepped into the warm water of the hot tub in her apartment complex, hoping to soothe the persistent knot in her back. Although the massage she had earlier in the week had provided some relief, the stresses of her day had brought the tension right back. She was uncomfortable using the communal spaces in her building, but the jets in her bathtub at home just weren't powerful enough to provide the deep muscle relaxation she needed, so she chose the slight discomfort of this more public space, even though the setting itself wasn't her preferred retreat. As she scanned the pool room to ensure she was alone, she felt a subtle unease; the idea of engaging in conversation with a stranger, especially after a day filled with constant dialogue—first with her patients and then with her own therapist—was far from appealing.

Once she confirmed she was alone, Charlotte allowed herself to relax. Leaning her achy back against a powerful jet, she closed her eyes and let her mind drift. She began to reflect on a patient she had met earlier that day—a young woman who had endured numerous suicide attempts, feeling utterly unsafe in her own body. Charlotte empathized deeply with the woman's pain and began to envision a treatment plan.

"Mind if I join you?"

Charlotte jumped at the coarse voice interrupting her thoughts. Her reaction startled the man who had approached her, causing him to take a step back. Realizing her response was excessive for the situation, she quickly apologized and moved aside, making room for the polite stranger. He cautiously entered the hot tub, seemingly aware that his presence had disturbed her. Sensing her reluctance, he intentionally created distance by positioning himself on the opposite side, and they sat in awkward silence.

Regret washed over Charlotte, and she berated herself for coming to the hot tub. This uncomfortable encounter only reinforced her aversion to using the facilities in her building. As she was contemplating a polite exit strategy, the man spoke up. "I didn't mean to startle you. I apologize. It seems like you wanted to be alone. I can leave if that's what you want."

Charlotte felt a wave of shame for making him feel unwelcome. After all, he had done nothing wrong. There was something about his gentle demeanor that suddenly put her at ease, momentarily reminding her of Adam. Adam had possessed the remarkable ability to make her feel safe. There was a unique connection between them, and their interactions flowed effortlessly. Since their separation, everything seemed to lose its meaning. A void remained unfilled, leaving her feeling cold and uncomfortable. Charlotte struggled to understand the emotional codependency she felt toward Adam; perhaps it was simply love. His presence had brightened her world, and his absence had plunged her into the darkest period of her life. Even now, three years later, she continued to grapple with finding the light.

As she sat in the hot tub with this stranger, a familiar comfort began to resurface. In this moment, she found herself torn between embracing the old, pleasant sensation—a comfort tinged with vulnerability and the potential for hurt—or defending the newfound comfort of distance, which, while unappealing, felt safe and protective.

Charlotte contemplated leaving the hot tub. Instead, she mustered a kind smile and introduced herself. His words, delivered with a gentle tone, washed over her, dissolving some of her initial irritation. They spoke for the next hour, gradually getting to know each other. His name was Michael, and he had a calm, unassuming presence that put her at ease. He spoke with a quiet confidence about his work as a graphic designer, his love for jazz, and the way he appreciated solitude—qualities that resonated with her own introverted tendencies. As their conversation deepened, Charlotte found herself sharing more than she intended, speaking briefly about her work and the challenges associated with it. Michael listened without judgment, offering a kind of understanding that made her feel seen and heard.

In that unexpected connection, Charlotte realized she was not yearning only for the comfort of the past, but also for the possibility of new, meaningful connections.

As Charlotte made her way back to her apartment later that evening, she felt invigorated. She realized that by welcoming back her vulnerability, she had made a powerful choice to surpass the safety of her comfort zone. Tolerating the discomfort had transformed it into something comfortable again, unveiling a potential new path for her—tolerating discomfort. She instinctively knew that this was the way to reclaim the fragmented parts of herself that had once disengaged.

Although the experience had been uncomfortable, Charlotte realized that enduring such discomfort was not just about stepping into challenging situations, but also about allowing herself to be vulnerable and open to connection. She understood that true healing and growth required her to face the very emotions and interactions she had been avoiding. It was in these moments of vulnerability—whether with herself or others—that she could begin to emerge from the darkness. The path forward was not just about placing herself in uncomfortable situations, but about embracing those moments as opportunities for connection, understanding, and ultimately, finding light where there once was only shadow.

Charlotte turned her thoughts back to planning her patient's care. She yearned to guide her toward feeling safe in her own body once more. The repetitive trauma had rendered life threatening, leading the woman to seek escape through self-destructive means. Charlotte understood that she needed to empower her patient, showing her the strength to confront potential pain instead of seeking to evade it. A new mode of being beckoned—a life not necessarily free of pain but one in which she possessed more power than the pain itself. This path would enable her to face adversity rather than avoid it.

Charlotte had dared to confront the confines of her mind, those boundaries erected not out of wisdom but as defensive ramparts shielding her from past vulnerabilities. This journey heightened her instinct for self-preservation, yet beneath the surface, she discerned a subtler truth: Her actions were driven more by a desire to evade than to heal. A deeper part of her, an elevated consciousness, acknowledged that her supposed protection was, in fact, an avoidance strategy, a fear of encountering fresh wounds. In this evasion, she realized the missed opportunities for self-discovery and genuine connections, yearnings that resonated deeply within her. The irony struck her forcefully; while she devoted herself to guiding others through similar inner labyrinths, she grappled with her own fears. This internal conflict, steeped in paradox, impelled her toward a crucial realization: In order to authentically help her patients, she needed to—fearlessly—explore her own barriers.

Out of habit, when Charlotte returned to her apartment, she headed straight to the medicine cabinet to retrieve a heat pack for her back. But, to her surprise, the knot had significantly improved. Had the pain subsided not only because of the physical relief of the soothing bubbles but also because she had dared to push against her comfort zone and reclaim a sense of self? The notion of regaining power brought a smile to her face.

Is Comfort Holding You Back from Growth?

In our pursuit of comfort, humans instinctively avoid anything that brings discomfort. Our brains are wired to dismiss unpleasant experiences and seek out situations and people that elicit positive emotions. This natural inclination to avoid pain is deeply ingrained within us. When faced with challenges, our instinct is to flee. However, those who have cultivated discipline from a young age understand that it entails doing what we do not naturally desire. By developing this ability, they build a higher tolerance for what others perceive as discomfort.

Athletes serve as a prime example of individuals who learn discipline at an early age. Most people lack the patience, commitment, and endurance required for the level of physical activity that athletes engage in daily. However, athletes are introduced to this demanding lifestyle from a young age, constantly pushing beyond their comfort zones. Over time, this becomes a learned skill that enables them to achieve feats that surpass what the average human body can accomplish.

Comfort and discomfort are not merely physical sensations but also psychological states. The body and mind are intricately connected, and when the body experiences discomfort, it signals the mind to stop. Similarly, when the mind interprets something as uncomfortable, it signals the body to respond accordingly. Paradoxically, change occurs when we reach the threshold of discomfort and surpass our existing limits.

After enduring trauma, protective responses emerge within us to shield ourselves from further pain. Just as a child runs away from the bark of a dog after being bitten, traumatized adults may consciously or unconsciously avoid potential pain. While this self-protective mechanism may serve them well during the healing process, they are faced with a choice: to reenter the playing field, risking potential hurt, or to remain on the sidelines, perpetually seeking safety but missing out on the game of life.

The brain of a traumatized individual continues to employ self-protective mechanisms, fleeing or dissociating from perceived threats, until a new association is formed with the source of pain. Similar to a child who gradually learns to trust dogs again through positive experiences that don't end in a painful bite, trauma work invites adults to embrace the discomfort of their past traumas, allowing for the possibility of a different response. This does not guarantee an absence of pain; rather, it entails a belief in yourself strong enough to not be consumed by the hurt.

Not every individual who experiences trauma will develop post-traumatic stress disorder (PTSD). Various factors influence the prevalence of trauma after an event, including the type and severity of trauma, demographic characteristics, and individual vulnerabilities. Traumatic events involving direct threats to life, serious injury, or sexual violence are more likely to lead to PTSD. Furthermore, preexisting risk factors such as a history of trauma, childhood adversity, or genetic predisposition can heighten a person's susceptibility to PTSD. Additionally, factors like a lack of social support, ineffective coping strategies, and certain biological factors may contribute to its development as well.

For individuals deeply affected by trauma, the primary goal is to understand that there's no assurance that the dog won't bite again. However, the objective isn't merely to avoid being bitten but to reshape the narrative by fostering the belief in our resilience to withstand a bite. The journey of overcoming trauma entails reclaiming the inner strength to trust in our ability to rise above the pain we endure. Healing commences with the realization that we possess the fortitude to endure the ordeal; we can then transition from a state of victimhood to one of survivorship.

A survivor mentality embodies resilience and determination in navigating adversity, marked by a steadfast belief in our capacity to overcome challenges. Associated with enduring discomfort, survivors recognize discomfort as a natural facet of life and a catalyst for personal growth. Rather than shying away from discomfort, they confront it head-on, viewing it as an opportunity for learning and development. Survivors tolerate short-term discomfort in pursuit of long-term goals, understanding that discomfort is transient and often precedes moments of growth and achievement. Embracing discomfort as a necessary step in the journey toward healing and self-actualization, individuals with a survivor mentality demonstrate courage and adaptability, thriving amid life's adversities.

Expanding Beyond Your Comfort Zone

To begin pushing through your comfort zone, it's important to reflect on what you might be missing by staying within it. Consider opportunities that have slipped by because you chose familiarity over the unknown. For instance, imagine being offered a chance to speak at a conference—a great opportunity to showcase your expertise and expand your network. If you decline because of fear of discomfort, you miss out on the potential professional growth and connections that could have followed. On the other hand, stepping outside your comfort zone could lead to new experiences, skills, and even unexpected successes, like gaining confidence and recognition in your field after delivering a successful presentation.

Fear and uncertainty often hold us back from trying new things, but these feelings can be reframed as opportunities for growth and learning. To turn discomfort into a learning experience, start by taking small, manageable steps. For example, if public speaking intimidates you, you might begin by speaking up more in smaller meetings, gradually building your confidence. Over time, these small steps accumulate, making it easier to tackle bigger challenges.

A shift in mindset can also help you embrace challenges and discomfort. Instead of viewing discomfort as something to avoid, try seeing it as a sign of growth—an indication that you're pushing your boundaries and expanding your capabilities. This mindset shift transforms challenges into opportunities to learn and grow, rather than obstacles to be feared.

As with every step of your healing journey, having a support system is crucial when stepping beyond your comfort zone. Think about who in your life can offer encouragement and accountability as you venture into new territory. Reflect on past experiences where stepping outside your comfort zone has benefited you, and write these down. This exercise not only reinforces your ability to grow but also provides motivation for future challenges.

Your core values and goals can serve as powerful motivators to push beyond your current limitations. Identify which of your goals require you to step into discomfort, and use these as guiding stars on your journey. Finally, it's important to celebrate and acknowledge your progress as you expand your comfort zone. You might do this by rewarding yourself after achieving a challenging milestone, sharing your success with a supportive friend, or journaling about your achievements. Recognizing your growth helps to reinforce your efforts and encourages continued expansion beyond your comfort zone.

8

Acceptance Versus Resignation

The morning greeted Charlotte with its breathtaking beauty, as the sky stretched out in an endless blue expanse. Today she had an appointment with her hairdresser at 9 a.m., a ritual she had scrupulously upheld as part of her broader effort to navigate this particularly challenging chapter of her life. This appointment represented more than mere self-care; it was a deliberate attempt to preserve a sense of normalcy, a way to anchor herself amid the emotional turbulence that had become a constant in her days. The routine provided a comforting structure, a familiar pattern she could hold on to as the world around her continued to shift and change unpredictably. Determined to fit in a spin class before her hair appointment, Charlotte had reluctantly decided to wake up early on a Saturday—the one day she could have slept in. Lying in bed, clutching her pillow, she peered out the window, searching for the motivation to leave the warmth and comfort of her cozy haven. The thought of facing another day felt daunting, yet she knew that occupying her time with activities was essential. The prospect of engaging with others—even those closest to her—felt overwhelming, so she chose instead the quieter solace of solitary routines. These personal rituals, though less demanding, provided her with the refuge she needed, allowing her to maintain a sense of balance and move forward, even as the emotional weight of her struggles pressed heavily on her.

As usual, her inner voices began their familiar dance. The encourager whispered, *Imagine how incredible you'll feel after the class, with all those endorphins flooding your system.* On the other hand, the discourager growled, *Who cares? I'm exhausted.* Charlotte knew she couldn't allow the discourager to win. Succumbing to that voice would feel like a personal defeat, and she despised losing. Reluctantly, she forced herself out of bed, determined not to let the discourager have the last word.

After her spin class, her body drenched in sweat, Charlotte silently praised herself for surpassing her goal of fifteen miles. Catching a glimpse of herself in the mirror, she couldn't help but hear the critical voice inside her head: *Did you really have to indulge in tiramisu after dinner last night? Where is your self-control?* Charlotte didn't have many vices, but her inner critic showed no mercy when it came to the few she enjoyed. However, her years of training and personal therapy intervened, reminding her, *It's okay. You deserve to unwind and indulge every once in a while. If a delicious dessert helps you achieve that, why not?* But the critic interjected, *You have no room for such indulgences*, leaving her momentarily speechless. Feeling defeated by her inner critic, Charlotte stepped into the shower, contemplating how, even after years of therapy, the critic still maintained such power over her. She resolved to address this issue with her analyst during their next session.

Nedia, her hairdresser, possessed a charm that was uniquely Lebanese, accentuated by her stylish bob. Charlotte admired Nedia's infectious energy and her ability to weave captivating stories without taking a breath. Throughout their interactions, Nedia had shared snippets of her own story—a tale marked by tragedy. She spoke of her mother's death during childbirth, her father's immediate remarriage, and the burden of her stepmother. At the age of eighteen, Nedia was compelled to marry one of her father's business partners, a man two decades her senior whom she loathed. Despite enduring the ravages of civil war, a revolution, and the heart-wrenching loss of her only child in a hotel explosion, Nedia radiated an unwavering zest for life.

Listening to Nedia excitedly discuss her upcoming trip to Peru, Charlotte couldn't help but marvel at her resilience. Life had dealt Nedia an unfair hand, yet she refused to let it consume her. While Nedia had been deprived of so much, she possessed an innate ability to find joy in what she had. Charlotte, on the other hand, seemed cursed with the opposite disposition; she had an uncanny knack for finding flaws in everything, robbing her of joy. She wondered how Nedia had managed to develop this positive attitude despite her hardships. How did she focus on what brought her happiness and avoid being swallowed by pain?

Before she realized it, the words escaped Charlotte's lips: "How are you not broken after enduring everything you have?" The room fell into an uncomfortable silence. The woman cutting a teenage girl's hair in the chair next to Charlotte cast her a disapproving look, making her realize that she had spoken those words much louder than she had intended.

Embarrassed, Charlotte found herself unable to cease her apologies—an ingrained habit she had acquired when she was just five years old. Nedia raised her hand, signaling Charlotte to stop, and reassured her. "It's okay. People ask me that all the time."

Trembling, Charlotte clasped her shaky left hand with her steadier right hand, attempting to quell her nerves. Not only had she failed to teach herself how to embrace the brighter side of life, despite years of training and personal therapy, but she had also unintentionally dampened the spirit of this courageous woman who had wholeheartedly embraced life despite her challenging circumstances.

In a comforting gesture, Nedia patted Charlotte on the shoulder and spoke in a gentle tone. "My darling, acceptance is like sitting in a field, gazing up at the sky, watching the clouds pass by, and becoming one with it all. There is no need to alter the moment. It's about observing the present. In this very moment, standing here with you, I know that I am okay. I also understand that life is a fleeting experience, encompassing both the good and the bad. I see it for what it is and acknowledge its lack of permanence. How can I take something so elusive seriously?"

Charlotte processed Nedia's words. Perhaps there was no predetermined meaning in an existence destined to perish. Maybe assigning significance to such a fleeting concept was futile, and the true goal lay in learning to appreciate and enjoy the journey itself. Charlotte envisioned how she often resisted the process rather than immersing herself in it and savoring each moment. The truth was, she didn't want to live life on life's terms; she wanted to shape life to fit her own desires. It was a battle she frequently lost. After all, life held far greater power.

The rest of the day, Charlotte continued to visualize Nedia's wisdom. She found herself stepping outside, gazing at the sky, and observing the ever-changing clouds. She attempted to simply be present with the unfolding process. There was an undeniable tranquility in doing so.

As Charlotte immersed herself in the practice of acceptance and observation, she began to realize that the true beauty of life lay not in trying to control or manipulate it but in surrendering to its natural flow. Her profound self-awareness revealed the depth of her fighter spirit, a resilient force that had weathered numerous storms in her life. This inner strength not only shielded her from yielding to adversity but also emboldened her to maintain trust and resilience amid daunting circumstances. Yet Charlotte recognized the nuanced nature of humanity; she understood that every aspect of her being harbored both light and shadow. This duality was evident in how her fighter spirit, while fiercely protective, could also manifest as hypercriticism toward herself, others, and the world at large. Despite her instinct to challenge and improve, Charlotte grappled with the realization that true navigation through life necessitated a delicate equilibrium between fortitude and acceptance. This nuanced understanding fueled her journey forward, inspiring her to seek a harmonious balance between her inner strength and the gentle art of letting things be.

When Should You Fight, and When Should You Let Go?

During times of hardship, we often find ourselves in one of three states: denial, coping, or thriving. Denial can lead to a dissociated existence. It deprives us of being fully present in our lives. It is a form of resignation, of allowing the bad to overwhelm the good. Coping, on the other hand, describes a semibearable life where one simply survives the process of life but with significant stress and a lack of ease, with an unusually escalated and reactive nervous system. This state often involves the fight-or-flight response. Thriving, the ideal state, allows individuals to prosper and flourish, without any escape or reactiveness; it equates with acceptance.

In the intricate dance of human responses to stress, three distinct physiological pathways emerge: the fight-or-flight response, the freeze response, and the ventral–vagal response.

The fight-or-flight response (surviving), a primal reaction to perceived threats, ignites a surge of adrenaline, elevating the heart rate and sharpening our senses to prepare for swift action. In contrast, the freeze response (resignation), orchestrated by the dorsal–vagal complex, induces a stillness—slowed heartbeat and breath—as the body seeks invisibility in the face of overwhelming danger. Meanwhile, the ventral–vagal response (acceptance), the embodiment of safety and connection, gently soothes frayed nerves, slowing heartbeats and promoting digestion, fostering a serene state conducive to restoration and social engagement. These three pathways, each finely tuned to its own purpose, reveal the remarkable adaptability and resilience of the human organism in navigating the ever-shifting currents of life's challenges.

The Buddhist perspective links acceptance with freedom in life. According to this view, the urge to control life is inconsequential. What truly matters is our capacity to observe life, rather than constantly seeking to manipulate it. Acceptance, therefore, is not propelled by action but by the capacity to observe without judgment. Within this lies the freedom of choice—the recognition that we aren't obligated to react in a specific way to something we dislike. Essentially, by embracing a phenomenon for what it is, we cultivate room to respond to it authentically, rather than striving to alter it into something else.

Acceptance is often misinterpreted as surrender. In defeat, one surrenders their power of choice and is bound to a predetermined reaction to a stimulus, which can feel confining and disempowering. Defeat tends to be more passive, leading us to either refrain from responding to the stressor, resulting in a sense of resignation and hopelessness, or to react negatively. On the contrary, acceptance empowers us to take control of a situation by intentionally choosing our response. The distinction between acceptance and mere survival lies in how we engage with the stressor: In survival we react, while in acceptance we respond thoughtfully and proactively.

Acceptance is often a subject of controversy, as it is frequently seen as defeat. In reality, it implies acknowledging that there are multiple ways to react to an undesirable situation. There is an element of willful surrender in acceptance, a willingness to observe rather than continually battle something that currently feels more powerful. Through observation, we open ourselves to discover what happens next.

Surrendering becomes a prerequisite for living harmoniously with oneself and others. The self-protection mode associated with fight-or-flight requires significant psychological and physical energy, often resulting in a constant feeling of overwhelm. Many psychological disorders, such as anxiety or depression, stem from the ongoing battle of coping with undesirable aspects of life.

Acceptance encompasses more than just a Buddhist philosophy; it involves navigating life with both a psychological and a physiological state of ease. To achieve this, we must develop the ability to consciously observe phenomena nonjudgmentally, without aversion to pain and the need to disengage from the undesirable. Growth is defined by fostering our ability to observe and embrace the full spectrum of experiences.

By practicing acceptance, we can cultivate a sense of peace and resilience, allowing us to navigate life's challenges with greater ease and harmony. Embracing life on our own terms involves actively asserting personal agency, making intentional choices, and aligning our actions with our individual values and aspirations. It emphasizes autonomy and self-determination in crafting our life path. Conversely, living life under life's terms involves acknowledging the inherent unpredictability and limitations of existence, accepting that certain circumstances are beyond our control. It requires cultivating resilience, adaptability, and acceptance in the face of adversity and uncertainty.

Despite their apparent differences, these approaches converge on the fundamental principle of embracing life with openness and authenticity. Both recognize the importance of acknowledging and honoring individual desires and values while also accepting the realities of life's unpredictability and impermanence. Ultimately, when done right, they work in harmony to guide us toward greater resilience, fulfillment, and contentment in the journey of life.

Empowering Yourself Through True Acceptance

Cultivating acceptance is a transformative process that involves a deep and ongoing reflection on your inner world and your responses to the adversities life presents. This journey often requires you to challenge deeply ingrained beliefs about yourself and the world around you, embracing a mindset of radical acceptance. Radical acceptance is not merely about passively enduring what comes your way; it is about fully acknowledging and embracing all facets of your experience—both the pleasurable and the painful—without judgment or resistance. This approach helps you to remain grounded in the present, letting go of the past and moving forward with intentionality and resilience.

One of the most effective ways to begin is through the practice of mindfulness, which encourages you to stay fully present with whatever arises in each moment. Mindfulness involves more than just paying attention; it's about cultivating a gentle, nonjudgmental awareness of your thoughts, emotions, and sensations. For example, you might start with a daily practice of mindful breathing—spending just five minutes focusing on your breath, observing it as it flows in and out of your body. When your mind inevitably wanders, you gently bring it back to the breath, allowing thoughts of the past or worries about the future to dissolve into the present moment. Over time, this practice can help you develop the ability to stay grounded in the present, reducing the grip of past regrets and future anxieties.

Incorporating mindfulness into routine activities can further deepen your practice of acceptance. Consider mindful eating, where you engage fully with the experience of eating—paying close attention to the flavors, textures, and sensations as you chew and swallow each bite. This practice not only enhances your connection to the present moment but also helps you cultivate a nonjudgmental attitude toward your experiences. By being present, you learn to embrace reality as it is, without the need to alter or escape it, which is a foundational aspect of acceptance.

Self-compassion is a cornerstone of radical acceptance, particularly when it comes to dealing with your own struggles and imperfections. It involves acknowledging that suffering and imperfection are part of the shared human experience and treating yourself with the same kindness you would offer to a dear friend. For example, after a challenging day where you feel you've fallen short, instead of berating yourself, you might practice self-compassion by acknowledging your efforts and understanding that everyone experiences setbacks. This could involve speaking to yourself with compassionate phrases like "I'm doing the best I can," or "It's okay to make mistakes; I'm learning." Such practices can soften your inner critic and support a more accepting attitude toward yourself, allowing you to embrace your imperfections without judgment and to move forward with a renewed sense of purpose.

In moments of intense difficulty, self-compassion can be deepened by engaging in practices that bring immediate comfort and relief. This might include placing a hand over your heart, taking a few deep breaths, and offering yourself words of kindness, such as "May I be strong in this moment," or "May I give myself the compassion I need." You could also create a self-compassion ritual, such as taking a warm bath or going for a walk in nature, where you focus on nurturing yourself without any agenda other than being kind to yourself. By regularly practicing these rituals, you build a reservoir of self-compassion that can be drawn upon in challenging times, reinforcing your capacity to accept yourself as you are.

Fear of uncertainty or change can be a significant barrier to acceptance. Overcoming this fear often involves embracing the discomfort that comes with stepping into the unknown. One strategy is to start by gradually exposing yourself to new situations, allowing yourself to experience small doses of uncertainty in a controlled manner. For instance, if you fear change in your professional life, you might begin by taking on a new project or learning a new skill that pushes your boundaries, all the while reminding yourself that discomfort is a natural part of growth. Positive affirmations, such as "I am capable of handling whatever comes my way," can also help reframe uncertainty as a challenge rather than a threat. Additionally, seeking support from others who have successfully navigated similar changes can provide reassurance and encouragement, making the process of embracing uncertainty feel less daunting.

Radical acceptance in relationships allows you to honor the differences and limitations of others while maintaining healthy boundaries. This approach fosters deeper connections based on mutual respect and understanding, rather than a desire to control or change the other person. For example, if a close friend or partner has a habit that irritates you, rather than trying to change them, you might practice accepting this aspect of their personality as part of who they are. By doing so, you reduce the tension in the relationship and open up space for greater empathy and connection. This doesn't mean tolerating behavior that crosses your boundaries; rather, it's about discerning what you can accept and what requires a firm boundary to protect your well-being.

Creating daily or weekly rituals that reinforce the practice of acceptance can serve as powerful reminders of its importance in your life. For instance, you might start each day with a few minutes of journaling, reflecting on the areas of your life where you are struggling to accept things as they are, and setting an intention to approach these challenges with an open heart and mind. Another practice could be creating a gratitude jar, where you regularly jot down moments of acceptance and gratitude and place them in the jar. Reviewing these notes periodically can remind you of the progress you've made and the benefits acceptance has brought into your life.

It's important to understand that acceptance is not about giving up or resigning to fate; it's an active choice to engage with life's challenges through openness and resilience. To reframe acceptance in this way, consider each challenge as an opportunity for growth. For example, when confronted with a difficult situation, instead of resisting it or wishing it away, ask yourself, *What can this teach me? How can I use this experience to strengthen my character?* By doing so, you transform acceptance into a dynamic process of learning and development, where every obstacle becomes a stepping stone toward greater wisdom and inner strength.

The positive aspect of this approach is that it empowers you to see challenges not as setbacks, but as opportunities for personal growth and transformation. This mindset shift allows you to approach life's difficulties with a sense of purpose and optimism, knowing that each experience, no matter how tough, contributes to your resilience and personal development. Acceptance, in this sense, becomes a powerful tool for building a more fulfilling and balanced life, where you are not merely surviving but thriving amid adversity.

9

Reaction Versus Response

Charlotte glanced at her phone in between her appointments and noticed several missed calls from the concierge of her apartment building. When she returned the call, the voice on the other end introduced herself as Tatiana, a name Charlotte could never quite remember. Tatiana's voice grew excited as she revealed the reason for the calls—multiple floral deliveries for Charlotte. Tatiana asked permission to deliver them to Charlotte's apartment, as they were taking up space in the office. Tatiana added, "You are a very lucky woman; somebody out there must really love you."

Charlotte's heart sank as soon as she heard Tatiana's words, immediately fearing that the flowers might be from Adam. The mere thought of him stirred a whirlwind of conflicting emotions that she had been trying to suppress. On one hand, there was a flutter of excitement—the kind that used to accompany every gesture from Adam when they were together. His grand, often unexpected displays of affection had once made her feel cherished and adored, feeding a deep-seated need for validation and love. The idea that Adam might be trying to win her back, to reclaim his place in her life, was undeniably alluring. It stroked her ego and reignited that part of her that had always yearned for his attention and approval.

But on a different level, as a psychologist, Charlotte was acutely aware of the unhealthy dynamics that had characterized their relationship. She understood that these gestures, while flattering on the surface, were often part of a broader pattern of emotional manipulation and control. This awareness made her uncomfortable, as it clashed with the part of her that still craved his affection. She wished, at times, that she could either be blissfully ignorant—able to simply enjoy the attention without seeing the darker undertones—or that she had the strength to decisively cut him out of her life once and for all.

She was neither ignorant nor able to fully sever the ties. Instead, she found herself torn between these two conflicting desires, actively trying to navigate her way through them. On one side, there was the thrill of being wanted and of Adam making an effort to reconnect, which momentarily filled the void his absence had left. On the other side, there was the rational understanding that allowing him back in, even in the smallest way, could unravel the progress she had made in moving on from him.

Charlotte was caught in this emotional tug-of-war, trying to find a path that would lead her out of this psychological maze, where old desires clashed with new boundaries, and where her head and heart seemed to be locked in an endless debate. Her reaction, then, was a complex mix of longing, fear, and the painful awareness that despite her outward composure, she was still very much under Adam's spell—a spell she desperately wished to break but couldn't fully escape.

Charlotte gave Tatiana permission to deliver the flowers to her apartment, and then turned her attention to the next patient entering her office.

At the end of her day, she looked forward to unraveling the puzzle awaiting her at home. Driving with a sense of urgency, a surge of excitement swept through her. She parked and hurried to the elevator, pressing the button repeatedly. When the elevator doors opened, she saw her hot tub neighbor inside. Charlotte couldn't have imagined a less opportune moment for an encounter. Although her primary desire was to reach her apartment, she engaged in polite conversation. However, she was distracted, eager to uncover the identity of her secret admirer. After the requisite small talk, she excused herself and rode the elevator up.

As she exited on her floor, Charlotte was struck by her neighbor's serene demeanor. There was something about him that quelled her inner turmoil. She couldn't pinpoint the exact quality, but she found herself immensely drawn to it. She put the thought aside as she slid her key into the lock, skipped into her apartment, and stopped short.

Her entire living room was adorned with purple hydrangeas, her favorite flowers. She knew without a doubt that Adam had sent them. Years ago, Adam had asked her about her favorite flowers. When she told him and he asked why, she had responded, "They possess an old-fashioned charm that is simply irresistible." In that tender moment, he pulled her closer and whispered, "So do you." The intensity of his gaze, his voice, and his touch caused the world to stand still.

As she looked around the room, she wondered, *What could this mean?* Her mind raced with conflicting thoughts. *Is he coming back? Has he finally realized what I've known all along—that we're meant for each other?* But even as these thoughts crossed her mind, she felt a sharp pang of doubt. She left Adam because she understood, deep down, that their relationship was toxic. While a part of her had always hoped he would change and they could somehow make it work, she also knew this was a dangerous fantasy—a remnant of the emotional grip he still had on her. Charlotte's heart was torn between this longing for the possibility that Adam had returned, finally ready to be the partner she had always wanted, and the rational understanding that his reappearance might only lead to more heartache. This internal conflict made her feel vulnerable, caught between the remnants of a love she couldn't fully let go of and the self-awareness that had driven her to leave him in the first place.

As she moved from one bouquet to the next, inspecting each vase for a card, her frustration began to build. There were at least fifty bouquets, placed on nearly every surface in the room. No wonder the office had been calling. But the absence of a note, a signature, or any clue as to who had sent the flowers only deepened her agitation. *How do you still manage to stir me up like this?* she muttered to herself. The mix of emotions—excitement, fear, hope, and dread—left her feeling more confused than ever. The flowers, whether a gesture of love or a reminder of the hold Adam still had over her, had thrown her into a spiral of emotions she wasn't prepared to face.

She made her way to the kitchen to fetch a glass of water. On her kitchen island sat the smallest bouquet of all, accompanied by a brief note that read, "Simply irresistible." Charlotte's heart sank again, as it had countless times that day. The card was unsigned, but she knew it was from Adam. She held it close to her chest, closing her eyes. She could almost sense his presence beside her, and just as he had said, it was simply irresistible.

She sat at the kitchen counter, her mind spinning with possibilities. If Adam was indeed trying to come back into her life—if the flowers and his visit were part of an effort to rekindle their relationship—what would that mean for her? Could she somehow forget the past and all the pain it held?

But she realized it wasn't just about forgetting; it was about forgiveness. Could she truly forgive Adam for the hurt he had caused her? And even if she could, would she be able to live with herself if she did? The memories of their tumultuous relationship and the emotional scars it left were not easily dismissed. On the other hand, could she continue living without him if she couldn't find it within herself to forgive? The thought of being without him again, after all this time, stirred a deep sense of uncertainty within her.

These questions had haunted her before, but they now held newfound urgency. Adam's renewed presence in her life, symbolized by the flowers and his unexpected visit, forced her to confront them head-on. The peace she had started to rebuild after their separation was once again disrupted, leaving her torn between the desire to protect herself and the lingering hope that maybe—just maybe—things could be different this time.

Charlotte couldn't shake the feeling that she had been doing just fine without him—at least on the surface. She had managed to move forward, albeit with the trauma from the accident still looming large. But Adam's return had reopened old wounds, bringing all the unresolved emotions to the forefront. The questions now bombarded her mind, demanding answers she wasn't sure she could provide. It wasn't as if she hadn't considered these questions before, but Adam's reappearance had brought them back with a force she couldn't ignore.

Then, the worst question of all surfaced in her mind. Did Adam truly want her back, or was this all merely a nostalgic trip down memory lane? A year ago, she had succumbed to curiosity and Googled his name, only to be met with a picture of him holding hands with a tall, beautiful blonde. In an instant, she shut her computer, vowing never to search for him again. The thought of him touching another woman churned her stomach, and despite only seeing the picture for a few seconds, it had been etched into her memory. She had often wondered if this woman was the cause of their breakup, and despite her best efforts, she hadn't been able to erase that image from her mind.

The last time she and Adam had been together as a couple, they strolled hand in hand toward the park, and the magic of the New York night diminished the pain of her heels. She leaned on his shoulder. He kissed her head and whispered, "I love your scent." Upon reaching the park, she darted toward the grass, shedding her shoes. Then she gazed upward, enchanted by the moon. Turning her attention to Adam, she found his gaze fixed upon her. She smiled, prompting him to approach, but he opted not to join her on the grass—a predictable choice. She blew him a kiss and said, "I'm thirsty!" She pointed with her chin toward a pretzel cart at the edge of the park.

In his stern manner, he chided, "You really should drink more water." He finally stepped onto the grass, then removed his jacket and handed it to her, pulling his wallet from the pocket before heading toward the cart.

Charlotte clutched the jacket close to her, careful to keep it off the grass, well aware of his sensitivity to such matters. As she shifted to place the jacket on her lap, his phone slipped from his pocket. As she leaned over to retrieve it and attempted to return it to its rightful place, the screen illuminated briefly.

She often wondered about the events that transpired that night, but all she could recall was an overwhelming sensation of pain. It was as if the pain had overridden her other senses and memories. A text message on the screen read, *Cannot wait to see you tomorrow night, my love. Miss you more than ever*, accompanied by three heart emojis. The sender's name was saved as TL.

Her world came to a halt. She looked down to reread the message, but the screen had gone black. She struggled to sit up, but her legs felt like jelly. A scorching heat enveloped her body, and everything seemed to accelerate beyond her ability to respond. The following moments were a blur, as if time had frozen. Nausea overwhelmed her, prompting her to stand, but her legs refused to cooperate.

Adam returned with a pair of water bottles and saw her distress. He lifted her up, concern etched on his face, and asked if she was all right. She gazed up at the man she had adored moments before. In that moment, Adam ceased to be the love of her life; instead, he'd become a predator who had violated her trust. Summoning all her strength, she pulled away from him.

He looked confused as she handed him his phone. He glanced at the screen, tilting his head back and closing his eyes. She stood there in silence. "It's not what you think," he murmured.

In a hushed whisper, she responded, "It's exactly what I think."

"I know it looks bad," he said. "I never meant to hurt you. You mean the world to me."

Her mind raced as she walked away, fully aware that there were no words he could offer in that moment to alleviate her anguish. The next thing she recalled was sitting barefoot in a taxi, clutching her shoes and Adam's jacket tightly, grappling with what she should do next. After all, how do you navigate a world that has crumbled around you? Charlotte had only one answer: Run. It was the sole method she knew to lessen the pain, to escape from the shattering reality that had engulfed her.

How to Stop Reacting and Start Responding Thoughtfully

A reaction is typically instinctual, immediate, and often driven by emotions, without much conscious thought or consideration of consequences. It can be impulsive and is often based on past conditioning or biases. In contrast, a response is more deliberate, thoughtful, and intentional. It involves taking a moment to assess the situation, considering various factors such as emotions, values, and goals, before choosing an appropriate course of action. Responses are typically proactive, guided by reason and reflection, and aimed at achieving a desired outcome or resolving a situation effectively.

When confronted with a perceived threat, individuals often rely on their survival instinct, which activates a defense mechanism aimed at self-preservation. This instinctual response, known as fight-or-flight mode, prompts individuals to either confront the threat head-on or seek to escape from it. These reactions occur swiftly and are rooted in unconscious beliefs, which may not always align with reality. For instance, someone with a history of being physically violated may instinctively perceive any unsolicited touch as threatening, triggering an immediate defensive reaction. Such defensive mechanisms develop as a result of past traumas.

It's crucial to acknowledge that negative reactions are frequently influenced by biased prejudices stemming from past beliefs, leading individuals to respond in a similar manner whenever they encounter similar situations, regardless of the actual circumstances. These reactions often become ingrained behavioral patterns that individuals consistently display, regardless of the justification for their reaction. In these cases, it is the amygdala within our emotional brain that reacts to specific triggers.

Conversely, a response represents a deliberate and mindful approach to addressing a stimulus that hasn't triggered a negative unconscious script. This response typically arises from the prefrontal cortex's capacity to objectively assess the situation and handle it without bias. In the aforementioned example, an individual without trauma may perceive unsolicited touch simply for what it is, enabling them to choose an appropriate response based on the circumstances. They might interpret the touch as friendly and nonthreatening, responding in a welcoming manner, or they may find it uncomfortable and take steps to address it. A response constitutes a well-justified reply rooted in unbiased information from both the conscious and unconscious mind. Responses generally tend to be less defensive and aggressive, unless genuine self-protection is warranted.

Reactions versus Responses

Reactions are guided chiefly by emotions, and responses stem from logical reasoning. While reactions often prolong disagreements, responses aim for conflict resolution. Reactions tend to provoke defensiveness and potential arguments, whereas responses nurture healthy discussions. Laden with past scripts, reactions may not suit the current situation, whereas responses are grounded solely in the present, unencumbered by past pain. Ultimately, reactions can leave both parties feeling frustrated and misunderstood, whereas responses foster a sense of growth and accomplishment.

In the realm of human interaction, a reaction manifests as an emotionally charged response stemming from unresolved experiences, while a response stands as mere feedback to the present moment. The pivotal ability to opt for a response over a reaction hinges on the power of choice. Regardless of circumstances, there is always a potential to exercise choice and respond in myriad ways, some more favorable than others. Making a conscious and constructive decision epitomizes the essence of choice. Self-awareness assumes a critical role in favoring response over reaction.

Nurturing self-awareness necessitates a mindful examination of your emotions in any given moment. But this endeavor requires liberation from unresolved past scripts that continue to govern the depths of the psyche. Recognizing fight-or-flight responses offers an avenue to reassess past scripts, thereby diminishing the propensity for reactionary behavior. As long as emotionally charged scripts persist in both the conscious and unconscious mind, reactions will endure. The journey toward transformation entails dissolving the emotional charge through inner work, ensuring these scripts no longer wield influence over our response.

Shifting from a reactive mindset to a responsive mindset involves a deliberate process of self-awareness and skill development. One key strategy is engaging in mindfulness practices, which can heighten your awareness of your thoughts and emotions, enabling you to recognize reactive patterns and choose more intentional responses. Emotional regulation techniques, such as deep breathing and relaxation exercises, help manage emotions in the moment, fostering a calm and thoughtful approach to situations. Cognitive restructuring, through questioning and challenging automatic negative thoughts, promotes more balanced and rational thinking. Taking a pause before responding allows time for reflection and evaluation, leading to more considered and effective responses. Developing empathy, problem-solving skills, and a mindset of patience and acceptance further strengthen the transition to a responsive mindset. Consistent practice and self-reflection play crucial roles in this transformation, empowering you to navigate challenges with resilience and compassion.

Mastering Challenges Through Mindful Response

Let's explore how to transform reactions into thoughtful responses using a consistent example throughout. Imagine you're at work, and in front of the entire team your colleague criticizes a project you've been working on. This scenario might trigger an immediate emotional reaction, but with practice, you can learn to respond thoughtfully instead.

Upon hearing the criticism, your initial reaction might be a surge of anger, embarrassment, or defensiveness. Instead of reacting immediately, however, try this: Pause and acknowledge what you're feeling. You might think to yourself, *I'm feeling angry and embarrassed because I wasn't expecting this critique.* By identifying your emotions, you begin to separate yourself from the intensity of the moment, creating the space needed to manage your response effectively.

The fact is that your colleague criticized your work publicly. However, you might be making assumptions like "They don't respect my work," or "They're trying to undermine me in front of the team." Recognize these assumptions and focus on what you know for sure. The actual criticism could be about a specific aspect of the project rather than a personal attack. This clarity helps you avoid reacting based on unfounded beliefs.

Reflect on your values, such as professionalism and integrity. Ask yourself, *How do I want to handle this situation in a way that aligns with my commitment to professionalism?* Instead of lashing out or becoming defensive, you might choose to respond by saying, "I appreciate the feedback. I'd like to discuss how we can address these concerns." This approach not only reflects your values but also helps maintain a positive work environment.

Reacting impulsively, such as snapping back at your colleague or dismissing their feedback, could damage your professional relationships or reputation. On the other hand, a thoughtful response that addresses the criticism constructively could lead to a stronger working relationship and an improved project. By considering these outcomes, you reinforce the importance of responding with care.

Before responding, take a moment to breathe deeply or ask for a short break to collect your thoughts. You might say, "I'd like to take a moment to think about what you've said and respond appropriately." This pause allows you to calm your emotions and approach the situation with a clearer mind, making it easier to choose a measured and effective response.

Consider your colleague's point of view. Perhaps they're under pressure from higher-ups or they genuinely want to see the project succeed and believe their critique is necessary. By thinking about these possibilities, you might approach the situation with more empathy and less defensiveness, allowing for a more constructive conversation.

When you're ready to respond, communicate your thoughts clearly and respectfully. You might say, "I understand you have concerns about the project. Could you clarify specific areas where you think improvements can be made? I'm open to making adjustments that will benefit the team." This response shows that you're taking the feedback seriously and are committed to improving the outcome.

If you find your emotions still running high, employ strategies to help regulate them. You might practice mindfulness by focusing on your breath, or you might recall a time when you handled a similar situation well to boost your confidence. These techniques help you stay calm and composed, even under pressure.

Empathy might lead you to say, "I can see that you're passionate about this project's success, and I appreciate that. Let's work together to address these issues." By acknowledging your colleague's perspective, you demonstrate understanding and a willingness to collaborate, which can help diffuse tension and promote teamwork.

Recall a previous situation where you reacted impulsively to criticism and how it affected the outcome. Maybe in the past, a defensive response led to a strained relationship with a colleague. Use that experience to remind yourself of the benefits of staying calm and constructive. In learning from the past, you can apply those lessons to respond more effectively in the present.

By following these steps and applying them to a consistent example, you can transform impulsive reactions into thoughtful, intentional responses. This approach not only helps you handle challenging situations with grace but it also strengthens your relationships and enhances your personal and professional growth. With practice, you'll find that responding thoughtfully becomes second nature, leading to more positive and productive interactions in all areas of your life.

10

True Versus False Self

Charlotte must have checked her phone every hour throughout the night. If you were to ask her, she'd say she wasn't even sure what she was waiting for, but there was a restlessness inside her, a yearning for something to happen. She woke up feeling irritable the next day and contemplated her schedule. She had the gym, a couple of patients, a lunch date with her sister, a few more patients, boxing, and a nail appointment at the end of the day—keeping busy as a way to be distracted from feeling. Her day seemed mundane, and she felt the urge to cancel everything and escape town. She felt disconnected from everyone and everything, but most importantly, she felt disconnected from herself.

She longed for something different, something more. The thought of change led her back to her living room. In the daylight, the flowers appeared even more enchanting. She gently touched the petals of the flowers in the vase on the counter. This sensory experience triggered a familiar train of thought. She realized that what she needed was a break, but it was more than that; she yearned for intimacy, the kind she had shared with Adam. She craved the rare pleasure of being in the presence of someone who made her feel intensely alive. To her, it was the epitome of mindfulness—a complete presence in the moment, without any concerns about the past or the future.

She decided to have breakfast on the balcony, in the fresh air. She settled into a comfortable chair, slipping off her slippers to feel the concrete beneath her feet. A gentle breeze welcomed her, caressing her skin. She closed her eyes and basked in the warmth of the sun. The combination of the moving breeze and the solid balcony beneath her feet provided a sense of containment she hadn't felt in a long time. It was as if something greater than herself was embracing her tightly. She searched her mind for the emotions she was experiencing, and all she could find was comfort.

Suddenly, she understood the significance of the phrase Mother Nature. She had heard it countless times before, but now she comprehended why it was called that. Nature had the power to embrace and nurture, like a loving mother. In that moment, despite her inner turmoil, she felt comforted, finding solace in the experience. She sat there for longer than she had intended, allowing herself to reconnect with her inner self. Then she realized a newfound excitement for her day. What had felt burdensome just an hour ago now seemed invigorating. This realization reinforced the understanding that whatever happens in her external world is simply a reflection of what is happening inside. When she is connected to herself, she can connect with life and find meaning in every experience. But when she loses that connection, nothing makes sense anymore, even things that once held great value for her.

From her work as a psychologist, Charlotte knew that this is what can happen when a person feels depressed. Her patients suffering from depression often shared their inability to find pleasure in everyday activities, a symptom referred to as anhedonia. In this state, individuals become so consumed by their pain that they lose the ability to derive pleasure from enjoyable experiences. Charlotte felt empathy for her patients when they expressed this feeling, yet in that moment, she realized something they struggled to see: No external change could bring back joy into a person's life when they were disconnected internally. They needed to shift their inner world.

The rest of the day went smoothly for Charlotte, aside from the unpleasant task of hospitalizing a patient against their will, which she always found challenging. However, her caseload was manageable and enjoyable.

She had arranged to meet her youngest sister, Laura, for lunch to celebrate Laura's recent triumph in a challenging legal case. The two women, both fiercely independent and strong-willed, had always shared a unique bond. Their similarities often led to spirited debates and the occasional clash, but beneath it all, they were each other's unwavering support system.

Over lunch, their conversation naturally drifted from celebrating Laura's success to the ongoing ordeal of their mother's affairs back home. Their mother, still living abroad, often required their joint efforts to handle everything from property management to navigating legal matters in their home country. Laura, with her legal expertise, often took the lead in handling complex issues, while Charlotte managed the more personal aspects, like ensuring their mother's comfort and well-being.

As they discussed the latest developments, from updating legal documents to coordinating their mother's healthcare needs, it was clear how much they relied on each other's strengths to keep everything running smoothly. Despite their occasional disagreements, their collaboration had always been seamless when it came to their mother—each understanding the other's perspective, even if they didn't always see eye to eye. This ongoing partnership, rooted in a deep familial bond, was a testament to their resilience and their shared commitment to their family.

After work, Charlotte headed straight to her boxing class. Boxing had been a passion of hers for the past ten years, and she loved it dearly. When people asked her about the appeal of boxing, Charlotte would explain, "It takes me away from all my weaknesses and puts me in a position of power." Despite her delicate appearance, she had a warrior spirit. She was strong, she recognized it, and she took pride in it.

Changing into her boxing gear, she began to warm up before the instructor arrived. Standing in front of the mirror, she started practicing her jabs and uppercuts, growing more intense and aggressive with each attempt. She gazed at the woman in the mirror—so strong and nearly invincible, yet so different from the way she sometimes felt inside. Adam had such a strong grip over her, and she wasn't strong enough to escape it. There was a part of her that felt disheartened, as if she had let herself down. Discontentment lingered within her, which she struggled to articulate to others and even to herself.

She examined the woman others described as tough and wondered, *If this is who I am, why do I sometimes feel so defeated? And if I am truly so weak, then who is this invincible woman staring back at me?*

She must have been lost in thought for a while because the next thing she knew, her instructor was yelling, "How long are you going to stand there? I don't have time to waste!"

Jolted back to the present, she snapped into action. The sharp words from her instructor propelled her into the workout, and she pushed herself even harder, determined to make up for the lost time and not let her mind wander again.

Charlotte left practice that night pondering which version of herself truly represented her essence and which was merely a false construct created as a defense mechanism due to her past wounds. She knew that, in order to feel truly fulfilled, she had to let her authentic self take charge. When she tapped into her power, nothing could intimidate or hinder her. Conversely, when she lost touch with it, she felt as though her world was collapsing. How could such contradictions coexist within her?

Once again, she wondered which version of herself was her true identity. Then she recalled reading somewhere that the great Roman emperor Marcus Aurelius had said, "Everything is a perspective, not a truth." That idea resonated with Charlotte. Neither of these states—powerful or defeated—was her entire truth, and therefore, neither was insignificant. Each perspective offered insight into who she was or, at the very least, who she had the potential to become. Overall, the process involved acknowledging all aspects of herself and transforming them into opportunities for personal development.

Each facet of her being held its own wisdom, offering profound insights when observed with openness. Even the aspects she perceived as weak contained valuable lessons. In a moment of inner harmony, she embraced all parts of herself without judgment or favoritism. This acceptance brought a profound sense of peace, as she recognized the beauty and value in her complete self.

Are You Living as Your True Self or Hiding Behind a Mask?

Donald Winnicott, an English psychoanalyst in the 1960s, introduced the concept of the false self versus the true self as a psychological theory. According to this dichotomy, the true self represents the authentic part of an individual that is fully engaged in life. It has the capacity to genuinely experience life and respond spontaneously to circumstances. On the other hand, the false self is a defensive facade that lacks vitality and may feel empty and disconnected in extreme cases.

Each of us possesses a sense of self that is a combination of both the true and the false self. However, the extent to which we were allowed to express our true self as children influences our authenticity as adults and the development of a solid sense of true self. In less than ideal upbringings, which is the case for most people, we are compelled from an early age to accommodate others and conform in order to survive. This compromise comes at the expense of our true self, leading us to grow into wounded adults whose personalities are largely governed by the false self.

The false self can be further characterized as the part of us that has evolved over time to ensure survival. Children instinctively understand that they need their parents' approval to sustain themselves, so they are willing to go to great lengths to obtain it. This often entails suppressing their true needs and desires. You could argue that the false self is constructed upon the repression of feelings deemed unacceptable by yourself or others.

When your false self dominates, you may experience distractions, confusion, indecision, resentment, irritability, criticism, anxiety, and depression. In order to empower your true self and maintain a more integrated mental state, you must have the courage to assess your needs and assert them, even if it disrupts the peace. Initially, such attempts may disturb the status quo and create chaos. However, they ultimately lead to greater self-awareness, balance, and joy.

To prioritize your true self, it is necessary to develop an awareness of your actualized needs through self-reflection. Recognizing the sacrifices you've made and their consequences can be deeply unsettling, as it allows you to identify the dysfunctions that hinder your experience of a more fulfilling life. This realization opens the door to potential change. These changes require considerable courage, because they often involve disrupting established patterns and reshaping your surroundings. Consequently, many of us sacrifice our true desires throughout life out of fear of the potential consequences of these changes. The hallmark of emotional maturity is found in your capacity to assert control over your needs and accept the inherent costs of living authentically.

However, the false self is not inherently negative. In fact, its formation possesses its own wisdom, and its integration is often necessary for adapting to life's demands. The goal is not to eradicate what is commonly referred to as the false self but rather to have it serve the true self instead of dominating it. A healthy false self acts as a loyal servant, finding socially appropriate ways to accommodate the true self's needs. In contrast, an unhealthy false self dominates by sacrificing the true self and perpetuating feelings of victimization and martyrdom. Therefore, the objective is to channel and regulate the false self for constructive purposes.

Our society places great emphasis on altruism and often criticizes the pursuit of our own needs as selfish. What is often overlooked, however, is the toll that self-sacrifice takes on each of us, leading to feelings of detachment, disengagement, and resentment. Even the most profound love cannot withstand long-term self-sacrifice without some form of psychological backlash. In order to truly value and appreciate others, it is essential to remain true to our own needs and desires.

It is vital for us to take stock of our genuine needs and seek healthy ways to fulfill them rather than suppressing them. By acknowledging and attending to our own needs, we create a foundation for authentic relationships and prevent the buildup of resentment or detachment that can arise from self-neglect. Balancing our own well-being with our relationships and commitments allows us to cultivate a sense of fulfillment and avoid the pitfalls of sacrificing ourselves for others.

This does not imply disregarding the needs of others or advocating for selfishness but rather recognizing the importance of self-care and self-awareness in maintaining healthy connections. It is a delicate balance that requires open communication, empathy, and mutual understanding. By valuing our own needs alongside the needs of others, we foster genuine connections and create a more harmonious and sustainable way of relating to those around us.

Discover Authenticity and Live Your Truth

To embark on the journey of activating your true self, begin with a deep reflection on your core values, beliefs, and passions. For example, if you find yourself consistently energized by helping others, this could point to a core value of service. Aligning with your true self means recognizing these moments of genuine fulfillment and ensuring that your life choices reflect these fundamental values.

Develop a morning ritual of reflection where you note down what feels most authentic to you. Over time, these notes will reveal patterns, helping you distinguish between passing interests and deeply held values.

In daily life, moments arise when your actions feel out of sync with who you truly are; these are moments of inauthenticity. For instance, if you find yourself agreeing with others just to avoid conflict, you might be suppressing your true self. Recognizing these instances is key to realigning with your authentic path. If your work environment stifles your creativity, for example, start by dedicating time each day to a creative project that reignites your passion. Gradually, these small adjustments will help you live more authentically.

We often wear masks to navigate social landscapes, but it's crucial to recognize when these facades start to suffocate your true self. For instance, you might find yourself adopting a serious demeanor at work even though you naturally have a playful personality. Recognizing this disconnect allows you to gradually let go of these masks. Begin by practicing authenticity in low-stakes environments. For example, share your true opinion in a casual conversation where the risks are minimal. Over time, extend this practice to more significant areas of your life, gradually shedding the layers of the false self.

The false self often manifests subtly in relationships and career choices. For example, you might constantly agree with your partner to avoid conflict, leading to resentment. Or you may have chosen a career path based on stability rather than passion, resulting in dissatisfaction. Start integrating small, authentic actions—such as expressing your true opinions in your relationships or exploring career options that better align with your passions. This gradual shift helps you reclaim your true self in these areas.

The false self is often a defense mechanism born out of fear—such as a fear of rejection or failure. For example, you might avoid pursuing a passion because you fear it won't be perfect. Confronting these fears involves acknowledging them and taking small steps to challenge them. Build resilience by starting small—like expressing an unpopular opinion in a safe space or pursuing a creative hobby without worrying about perfection. These small acts of courage can gradually dismantle the false self.

Your True Self

To fully activate your true self, you must embrace the parts of you that have been hidden or suppressed. For example, if you've been critical of yourself for not achieving certain goals, practice self-compassion by acknowledging your efforts and progress, no matter how small. If you've suppressed a creative side because you feared it wasn't "good enough," start by creating just for the sake of expression, without judgment. Celebrate the act of creation itself as an authentic expression of your true self.

Your true self flourishes in environments and activities that resonate with your authentic being. If you feel most alive when engaging in creative pursuits or spending time in nature, make these activities a regular part of your life. If painting or writing brings you joy, set aside time each week to engage in these activities. Surround yourself with people and environments that encourage and nurture your true self, rather than those that demand conformity.

The journey to the true self requires releasing the need for external validation. For example, if you've been making decisions based on what others expect of you, consider what your life would look like if you made choices based solely on your own values and desires. Start making decisions that align with your internal compass, such as pursuing a career or hobby that fulfills you, even if it doesn't meet societal norms or others' expectations. This practice helps diminish the need for external approval, allowing your true self to emerge.

This journey is not linear, nor is it easy, but it is profoundly rewarding. By consistently reflecting on your core values, acknowledging inauthenticities, and taking small steps toward a more authentic life, you activate your true self. This path demands courage, self-compassion, and a willingness to confront fears, but it ultimately leads to a life that is deeply aligned with who you truly are—one filled with purpose, fulfillment, and genuine connection.

11

Self-Destruction Versus Self-Construction

On a brisk Wednesday afternoon, Charlotte found herself nestled in her oversized leather chair in her Los Angeles office, immersed in taking notes about her previous patient. While it was her least favorite part of the job, she had discovered a way to make it more bearable by listening to the Three Tenors' London concert from 1996. The familiar melodies and powerful voices never failed to uplift her spirits, transporting her back to the cherished memory of attending the actual concert with her father. Though distant, it held a special place in her heart.

She took a sip of tea and peered out the window at the gently changing foliage. There was something about autumn and singing voices that stirred a sense of nostalgia within her. Perhaps nature shedding its leaves reminded her that letting go of what no longer serves us is essential for growth and renewal.

Charlotte's mind wandered, grappling with the past that seemed to hold her captive. The resonant voices of the tenors cast a reflective shadow down memory lane, stirring both fond and painful recollections. She found herself engulfed in the memory of a specific night. At eighteen years old, she had been brimming with innocence and hope, oblivious to the trials life would soon unveil. Tears welled up in her eyes as she thought of her father, a towering figure. She often pondered whether her perception of him had been colored by his being her father or whether he truly possessed such a formidable presence. Regardless, he had been her universe, a beacon of solace and protection.

His passing had irrevocably altered everything. The loss of her father had etched a profound grief within her, a wound that time had not entirely salved. Despite her efforts to come to terms with his absence, she felt incomplete. Charlotte yearned to reclaim the sense of security and comfort that his presence had once given her. It was as if a part of her had vanished alongside him, leaving an aching emptiness. She knew deep down that she needed to relinquish the pain of her past and focus on her future.

With the music still playing softly in the background, Charlotte wiped her tears and drew in a deep, steadying breath. She vowed to embrace the ever-changing seasons of life, to honor her past without allowing it to define her. It was time to release, to find solace within herself, and to craft a future that resonated with her true desires and aspirations.

Reminiscing about a trip she had taken with her father brought a bittersweet mix of emotions for Charlotte. She cherished his silliness, imitating the tenors as they sang. Though she'd just turned eighteen, her father had told her, "You're not officially an adult until you've heard the tenors sing in person." He had taken her on the most memorable trip to London; from their luxurious suite at the Dorchester to the unforgettable dinner at Quaglino's before the concert, her father had made every moment special. One particular keepsake she treasured was the formal gown he had surprised her with during their visit to Harrods, a symbol of his thoughtfulness and love that she still held on to after all these years. He had a knack for living life to the fullest, and Charlotte admired his ability to appreciate life and create lasting memories.

From Charlotte's perspective, people fell into two distinct categories: those who blended in and those who radiated an electrifying energy, leaving a lasting impression wherever they went. The former were adept at navigating with ease, appreciated by many for their ability to maintain harmony and adhere to conventions. The latter defied the status quo, possessing a potent and often dramatic aura. They garnered both admiration and disdain for their inclination to forge their own path and eschew conformity. Undoubtedly, her father belonged to the latter category—a dynamic force of nature whose vibrant energy left an indelible imprint on everyone around him.

Yet, Charlotte understood that people were rarely as straightforward as they seemed on the surface. She'd come to realize that each person carried a duality within them, a blend of both light and dark. As her father's vibrant energy was unmatched, so too was his capacity for intensity and volatility. This duality was a concept she'd encountered in the work of Carl Jung, who believed that every energy, every trait, holds its opposite within it. Kindness, for instance, could reveal its counterpart of unkindness, as even the brightest light casts shadows.

Her father was a striking embodiment of this idea. His charisma and charm were undeniable, yet beneath that brilliance lay wounds that shaped his behavior in unexpected ways. Much like Charlotte, he had endured a life-altering tragedy—losing his own father in a car accident when he was just a boy. The devastating loss left him grappling with the responsibility of caring for his grieving mother and younger siblings, thrusting him into adulthood far too soon.

The experience was profoundly traumatic, etching emotional scars that remained with him even as he grew into a man of great influence and inspiration. As much as he uplifted those around him with his wit and presence, he carried within him a streak of destructiveness—a shadow of his unresolved pain. Charlotte recognized that these unhealed wounds not only added depth to his character but also served as stark reminders of how the echoes of past trauma could surface in unexpected, often darker ways.

This understanding of duality was both a revelation and a comfort to Charlotte. It reminded her that no one, not even someone as exceptional as her father, was entirely one thing or another. People, she realized, were mosaics of contrasting energies, and it was in the acknowledgment of these contradictions that true understanding and compassion were born.

Despite the overwhelming grief and monumental challenges ahead, her father embraced his responsibilities with determination and a profound sense of love. He emerged as the cornerstone for his grief-stricken mother and siblings, offering solace and support during their darkest moments. Assuming the helm of the family business, he ensured the essential needs of the family were met. While Charlotte harbored doubts about the family's complete adaptation to the sudden loss, she held steadfast in her admiration for her father. Despite being merely a young boy at the time, he had marshaled all available resources to aid his family during their time of need, embodying resilience and fortitude beyond his years.

Charlotte could sense his pain when she was a child, although she lacked the understanding to articulate it at the time. He struggled to control his anger. While his constructive side was undeniably powerful, he exhibited the same intensity of destruction.

Deep inside, Charlotte knew that she had inherited some of her father's power, and she recognized moments when it surfaced, both to her advantage and detriment. She understood that power, when used unwisely, could be dangerous. In her youth, she had tried to suppress this aspect of herself. However, as she grew older, she realized that this power was a gift and she needed to learn how to wield it wisely. Disregarding it was not an option; instead, she had to navigate and channel it effectively. The goal was to tame this less-refined part of herself, learning to apply it in a way that benefited both herself and others.

As she gazed at the barren trees, a sense of readiness washed over her. She was prepared to work on managing the destructive side of her inherited power, even though she didn't yet know exactly how. The idea of trying was both liberating and enticing, akin to leaving behind the burdens of her past and embracing a new path forward.

How Do You Stop Self-Sabotaging and Build Constructively?

Among the complexities of human behavior, a common thread emerges: Emotional pain often acts as a catalyst for self-destructive tendencies. Individuals grappling with overwhelming emotions frequently turn to coping mechanisms designed to dull or alleviate their distress. These behaviors, though diverse in their manifestations, share a common origin in the struggle to navigate inner turmoil. Self-destructive actions can provide temporary relief from intense emotions or serve as a means to compensate for a sense of disconnection from oneself and others.

These behaviors encompass a spectrum, ranging from subtle forms of self-regulation like overworking and excessive exercise to more overt expressions such as substance abuse, risky sexual behavior, compulsive gambling, compulsive shopping, infidelity, self-harm, and involvement in abusive relationships. Each action reflects a unique attempt to manage internal turmoil and regain a sense of control, albeit through destructive means.

Self-destructive behavior includes actions that hinder personal growth and carry the potential to harm the individual. In contrast, self-constructive behavior refers to actions that, despite their initial discomfort, ultimately contribute to personal development and growth.

Irrespective of the chosen activity, self-destructive behavior generally originates from unconscious, compulsive impulses rather than deliberate, rational thought processes. While it may offer temporary relief, it frequently leads to heightened feelings of emptiness and distress, compelling us to pursue further actions in a bid to ease the anguish. This addictive cycle poses significant obstacles to thriving and undermines our efforts toward personal growth.

In contrast, self-constructive behavior is characterized by conscious intention and purpose, embodying a sincere commitment to personal growth and self-improvement rather than a reactive response to emotions. By engaging in constructive behavior, we can actively tap into our latent potential, essential for thriving, fostering heightened awareness, and making progress. However, pursuing constructive paths necessitates learning to endure the discomfort inherent in growth.

Between the stimulus and our response lies an imaginary gap, where we face a pivotal choice: whether to engage in constructive or destructive behavior. When discomfort arises from an event, we find ourselves in a liminal space of decision-making. Here, we can either succumb to our emotions, seeking escape or destruction, or cultivate the ability to tolerate them, paving the way for more nuanced and mature responses.

Switching from Destructive to Constructive Acts

The transition from destructive to constructive behavior hinges on our growing capacity to tolerate not only our own emotions but also those of others. As we enhance our ability to sit with the raw experience of emotion, we gain the power to process it into something more manageable, empowering us to respond with wisdom and effectiveness. Conversely, when events profoundly shake us, our connection to our higher self can falter, bypassing the rationality of our logical brain. This bypass often leads to heightened activity in the midbrain, triggering emotional reactions that may manifest as self-destructive coping mechanisms in response to unwanted emotions.

Our brains are deeply shaped by past experiences, unique strengths, and the information we encounter in our environment—all of which program our minds to respond in specific ways to various situations. Each of us possesses a repertoire of reactions to triggers, with some being more optimal than others. Nonetheless, all humans exhibit a spectrum of responses that range from functional to dysfunctional at times. Due to this learned behavior, our brains tend to default to familiar patterns unless we intervene to introduce something new into the mix. Consistently providing the same response to a stimulus solidifies those neural pathways.

For example, think of the common reaction of becoming defensive when receiving constructive criticism. If, in the past, criticism was often met with negative outcomes—like judgment or punishment—our brains may have learned to associate criticism with threat, triggering a defensive response automatically. Over time, this response becomes ingrained, even in situations where it isn't productive or necessary, such as during supportive feedback from a friend or colleague.

However, creating space for different responses allows for the recognition of new potential pathways, fostering new and more constructive reactions. We don't necessarily want to disrupt our functional responses, because they serve us well and do not result in self-destruction. It's the dysfunctional responses that pose harm to us. Therefore, the initial step involves identifying these dysfunctional responses to phenomena and evaluating how frequently we engage in them.

After identifying these dysfunctional responses, the next step is to focus on creating an imaginary stop button between our triggers and responses, pushing it each time to instigate a pause. During this crucial pause, the objective is to engage in as many functional activities as possible, meticulously assessing which ones could effectively supplant the negative ones. Optimal results stem from maintaining a functional state consistently. This vigilance is essential, because the emotional brain possesses the propensity to overshadow our logical faculties during moments of distress. Through the internalization of these constructive habits, it becomes second nature to implement them when confronted with moments of turmoil.

Transforming Destructive Patterns into Constructive Growth

To shift focus from self-destruction to self-construction, begin by identifying actionable steps that can immediately contribute to a healthier and more fulfilling life. For instance, if you struggle with negative self-talk, one way to transform this into constructive self-talk is by practicing daily affirmations. Start by acknowledging your strengths and setting positive intentions for the day, such as "I am capable of handling challenges," or "I deserve to take care of myself." If you often find yourself thinking, *I can't do anything right*, consciously replace that thought with *I am learning and growing every day*. Over time, this practice will help rewire your thinking patterns, shifting from a destructive to a constructive mindset.

Developing healthy routines can also promote self-care and well-being. For example, establish a morning routine that includes activities like meditation, exercise, or journaling. These practices not only improve mental health but also create a sense of structure and stability, helping you start the day with a positive mindset.

Consider past challenges as valuable lessons that have strengthened your resilience. Reflect on a difficult situation you've overcome. How did you manage to get through it? What skills did you develop as a result? By reframing these experiences as opportunities for growth, you can turn setbacks into stepping stones. If you face an obstacle in your career, use it as a motivation to acquire new skills or further your education. Define clear, actionable goals, such as enrolling in a course that aligns with your career aspirations, or setting up a networking plan to connect with professionals in your field.

To cultivate a positive mindset, practice gratitude daily. This could involve writing down three things you're grateful for each evening, which helps shift focus from what's lacking to what's abundant in your life. Embrace setbacks as learning experiences by asking yourself, "What can I learn from this?" rather than dwelling on the failure.

Using available resources and support systems is crucial for personal development. This might involve seeking out a mentor, joining a support group, or working with a therapist to guide your journey. Online courses, self-help books, and workshops can also provide valuable knowledge and skills. If you're looking to enhance your emotional intelligence, consider exploring relevant online courses or reading self-help materials that focus on mindfulness. These tools can equip you with the skills needed to navigate challenges constructively.

Forgiveness is a powerful tool in building a brighter future. Start by acknowledging past mistakes and recognizing that they are part of your growth journey. Letting go of regrets frees up emotional energy that can be redirected toward positive endeavors.

If you've been holding on to guilt over a past decision, write a letter of forgiveness to yourself. This act of self-compassion helps to release the burden of the past, allowing you to focus on the future.

Make self-love and self-compassion the foundation of your self-construction efforts. This means treating yourself with kindness, setting boundaries to protect your well-being, and engaging in activities that nourish your soul. Regularly schedule "me time," where you engage in activities that bring you joy, such as reading, taking a walk in nature, or practicing a hobby. This reinforces the importance of self-care and helps sustain your efforts toward personal growth.

Transforming self-destructive behaviors into self-constructive actions is a process that requires intentionality, patience, and support. By incorporating daily practices that promote positive thinking, leveraging past challenges for growth, and using available resources, you can build a life that resonates with your true values and aspirations. Remember, this journey is ongoing, and each small step contributes to a larger transformation toward a more fulfilling and authentic life.

12

Desire Versus Pain

Charlotte rushed through the crowded gate, apologizing profusely to the people she bumped in line, fearing she would miss her flight. Being late was highly unusual for her, and she couldn't believe she had overslept that morning. Finally reaching the gate, she breathed a sigh of relief as she handed her boarding pass to the airline officer, who informed her that she was the last passenger. Still catching her breath, Charlotte settled into her seat, removing her coat and trying to calm her racing heart after the close call.

She was en route to London for a lecture on the psychology of regulation at the Tavistock Institute. It was also an opportunity to spend time with her sister and enjoy the city she held dear. Requesting a cup of tea, Charlotte made herself comfortable, contemplating her itinerary and the activities she looked forward to. The thought of reconnecting with her sister brought a genuine smile to her face, despite their differences.

Charlotte's anticipation of seeing Kara again was clouded by the recent violation of her privacy when her sister had given Adam her address without consulting her—which had shaken her trust and left her feeling exposed. However, Charlotte's deep commitment to family and her unwavering love for her sister outweighed the hurt she felt. Her sister meant the world to her, and Charlotte valued their relationship too much to let this incident create a lasting rift. While the wound was still fresh, Charlotte was determined to focus on the bigger picture. Despite the uncomfortable tension that now lingered between them, Charlotte knew that her sister's mistake was a momentary lapse in judgment, not a reflection of her character or of the bond they shared. As much as it hurt, Charlotte believed in the strength of their connection and was resolved to find a way to move past it, knowing their relationship was worth more than the pain it had caused.

As the flight attendant announced takeoff, Charlotte decided to close her eyes and unwind from the rushed morning. Although she rarely managed to sleep on planes, she hoped to at least rest for a while. Drifting into an alpha state, that blissful realm between wakefulness and slumber, she felt a tender caress, as if a gentle hand brushed her hair away from her face. Uncertain if she had drifted into a dream, Charlotte perceived the touch with a curious serenity, devoid of any sense of intrusion. It was enigmatically familiar, a sensation that ensnared her consciousness.

Opting to keep her eyes closed, she yearned to relish that emotional connection once more. It felt comforting and inviting. However, moments passed without any further sensation, and the flight attendant's announcement drew her attention, prompting her to open her eyes. Deciding that the touch must have been a pleasant dream or illusion, Charlotte's gaze landed on a passenger nearby, and her senses momentarily froze.

There he was—Adam—gazing back at her with that familiar smile that had always melted her heart. In that instant, a less healthy part of her felt a surge of happiness, clinging to the hope that maybe, despite everything, this was it—the moment they could begin again. This part of her had been holding on since the flower delivery a few weeks ago, longing for his reappearance, feeding on the fantasy that he would realize what they could still have together. The sight of him reignited this lingering hope, bringing a mix of joy and a familiar ache, as if his presence was the answer to the unresolved longing she had been carrying.

At the same time, a healthier, more rational part of her—the one shaped by her years of psychological practice—recognized the danger in this moment. This part knew that the emotional attachment she felt wasn't based on love alone but was tangled with nostalgia, fear of letting go, and the comfort of the familiar. It reminded her of the reasons they had parted, of the pain that had followed, and urged caution in the face of his unexpected return.

Caught between these two forces—one yearning for the happiness and hope that his presence brought, and the other warning her of the risks—Charlotte felt the intensity of the internal battle. She trembled as Adam made his way toward her, covering herself with the neatly placed blanket in an attempt to regain her composure. The struggle between the desire to embrace this moment and the need to protect herself from further pain raged within her, leaving her unsure of which path to follow.

Charlotte watched as Adam approached her seat, and a mixture of emotions surged within her. Part of her wanted to flee, knowing that she lost control when he was around. He had a mysterious hold over her, as if he possessed the power to hypnotize. Despite her better judgment, she remained seated, waiting for him. In that moment, she wished to freeze time and savor the potential anticipation, longing, and desire. Her heart raced faster and faster as he drew nearer, until he was right beside her, within touching distance. Leaning over, he planted a kiss on her cheek and lingered close, confirming that it was indeed he who had brushed her hair earlier. The intense pleasure she experienced suddenly made sense; she wasn't dreaming. His face remained near hers, his breath mingling with hers, both elevated and heavy.

Reaching for her hand, he whispered in her ear, "My God, I have missed you." Charlotte sat motionless, holding her breath, afraid to make a move or utter a word. She simply absorbed every second, etching it into her memory.

Summoning her courage, Charlotte finally broke the silence, her voice a delicate tremor against the hum of the airplane cabin. With her eyes closed, she tightened her grip on his hand and murmured, "It's always nice to be missed." The words were carefully chosen, a blend of vulnerability and guardedness, revealing a part of her that still yearned for his attention, even as she grappled with the implications of his sudden reappearance. It was an admission veiled in subtlety, reflecting the complexity of her emotions—emotions that she wasn't entirely ready to confront.

Adam's response was immediate, though understated. He withdrew his hand, the physical distance between them widening as he retreated slightly, creating a small but significant space that seemed to mirror the emotional chasm between them. His eyes remained locked on hers, probing, searching for something she wasn't sure she wanted to reveal. Their exchanged glances held a bittersweet mix of admiration and sorrow, a silent acknowledgment of all that had been and all that could never be again—emotions known only to the two of them, shaped by the history they shared and the unspoken tension between them.

"You didn't miss me?" Adam's question was more than a simple inquiry; it was a challenge, a subtle provocation that sought to unearth the truth buried beneath her composed exterior.

Charlotte hesitated, her mind swirling with thoughts she couldn't fully articulate. *Missing doesn't even begin to describe what I felt for you*, she mused inwardly, but she couldn't bring herself to say it aloud. Instead, she deflected, her voice tinged with a mix of surprise and guarded curiosity as she asked, "What are you doing here?"

Adam took a step back, though in the cramped confines of the airplane aisle, the movement looked more like a retreat, a subtle acknowledgment of the boundaries that now existed between them. His original seat had been a few rows away, a fact that made his presence beside her all the more deliberate. He stood over her, his figure imposing in the narrow space, a crooked—and all too familiar—smile playing at the corner of his lips. It was the same smile he wore whenever he had done something he knew would draw reproach, a disarming yet infuriating expression that hinted at his awareness of the effect he still had on her.

Eventually he whispered with a hint of mischief, "Do you want the truth, or can I lie my way out of this one?"

The words, though playful in tone, sent a chill down Charlotte's spine. There was something unsettling in the way he so casually toyed with the truth, as if honesty was just another option, not a necessity. Tilting her head to the side, she simply stared, her expression carefully neutral, a silent challenge for him to drop the pretense.

His smile faltered, and after a moment, he relented. "Fine. Your sister told me you were flying to London today. I also had some business there, and I thought the plane would be the best place to get you to listen to me without running away." He emphasized his words with that same familiar smile, adding, "Unless you hate me enough to jump out of a flying plane. The choice is yours."

As a therapist, Charlotte was keenly aware of the dynamics at play—Adam's subtle, deliberate attempt to exert control using the guise of charm. The way he casually manipulated the situation, with his disarming smile and seemingly innocuous words, was all too familiar. His approach was calculated, designed to make her feel cornered, as if there were no escape from the conversation he wanted to force upon her. The airplane's confined space and their shared history provided the perfect backdrop for his subtle but unmistakable power play.

Despite her professional insight, Charlotte found herself battling a storm of emotions. Her instincts, honed over years of experience, allowed her to dissect his behavior with clinical precision. But she wasn't merely a therapist in this moment; she was a woman wrestling with the shadows of a relationship that had once defined her. The part of her that had cradled the memory of him since the flower delivery weeks ago now struggled to reconcile the Adam before her with the reality of his calculated actions.

The discord between her understanding and her feelings created a tension that threatened to unravel her. Could she be so entangled in the unresolved threads of their past that she might overlook the clear signs of manipulation? The notion was as sobering as it was terrifying. The person she had become—the one who had painstakingly rebuilt her life—could not afford to slip back into the patterns that once held her captive.

As this realization settled over her, Charlotte couldn't help but smile at the irony. *I wish I could hate you*, she thought. *My life would be so much easier*. But all that escaped her lips was a passive-aggressive "I think I'll take my chances with jumping" as she pretended to rise from her seat.

Adam burst into laughter and took a step closer. Her heart raced as he approached, a mix of excitement and dread surging through her body. Just as she was getting up, the plane shook with turbulence, nearly causing her to lose her balance. In that split second, he reached out to steady her, and their eyes locked once again. The familiar pull between them became impossible to ignore, a magnetic force that drew them together despite the logic against it screaming in her mind.

As he pulled her closer and embraced her tightly, Charlotte's resolve wavered. Unable to resist, she closed her eyes and reciprocated the embrace, holding him as tightly as she could. Tears began to stream down her face, a physical manifestation of the emotional battle raging within her. The surrounding passengers watched as Charlotte and Adam stood locked in each other's arms—a poignant image of love, pain, and the complexity of human connection.

Even as she held him, Charlotte was painfully aware of the internal conflict—the part of her that longed for this connection, for the comfort of what was familiar, and the part that knew better, that understood the dangers of falling back into old patterns. The turbulence outside mirrored the storm within, but in that moment, she allowed herself to feel the full weight of her emotions, knowing that the battle was far from over.

She finally pulled back slightly, just enough to look him in the eye. "Adam," she began, her voice both firm and steady, "you don't need to trap me to talk to me. If you have something to say, say it. But I won't be manipulated into listening or responding the way you want me to."

His smile wavered, a flicker of something unreadable passing through his eyes. For a brief moment, he seemed to grasp that the woman standing before him was not the same Charlotte he once knew. The power dynamic between them shifted subtly, as Charlotte reclaimed a part of herself that he had once tried to control.

The remainder of the long flight to London passed by in a blur, the hours slipping away as Charlotte and Adam engaged in a continuous, lively conversation whenever allowed by the flight crew or during moments when they were free to leave their seats. They navigated the safer waters of careers, world politics, family updates, travel stories, and future aspirations—anything tangible that allowed them to skirt the edges of the emotional quagmire that lay beneath the surface. The topics were carefully chosen, deliberate in their avoidance of the past and their romantic history, as if by mutual, unspoken agreement. To an outside observer, it might have seemed like two old friends catching up after years apart.

Despite the flow of their conversation, there were moments when a flight attendant would pause by their row, gently reminding Adam to return to his seat. Each time, he would make a casual excuse, mentioning how the two of them were discussing something important, his tone so effortlessly charming that the attendant would reluctantly move on, leaving him to remain by Charlotte's side. It was as though Adam had decided that, for the duration of this flight, he belonged there, and Charlotte couldn't quite bring herself to send him away.

In a rare moment of silence, Charlotte found herself reflecting on the conversation that had unfolded. There was a familiarity to it that she hadn't realized she missed—a rhythm to their exchange that felt both comforting and disconcerting. Yet beneath the surface of their easy rapport, she recognized the layers of complexity that made this interaction far more nuanced than it appeared.

She couldn't help but wonder why she still held Adam in such high regard. He had betrayed her, failed her as a partner in the most fundamental way, and yet here she was, valuing his opinions, yearning for his presence. It was a realization that unsettled her. Perhaps it was the ghost of the man he once was—the man she had once loved deeply, before the trust was shattered—that kept her tethered to this complicated connection.

As they spoke, Charlotte realized that it wasn't just the idea of him as a partner that she longed for; it was more than that. She missed the essence of him—the way his mind worked, the way his presence could fill a room, the intellectual sparring that had once been the foundation of their relationship. It was these things that had captivated her, that had made her fall in love with him in the first place. But now, with the clarity that distance and time had afforded her, she saw the complexity of their reality—two people connected by history but irrevocably changed by the choices that had led them here.

She felt the familiar pull of the past, the allure of what once was, but she also knew that neither of them were the same people anymore. The conversation was a reminder of what they had shared, but it also underscored the intricate and often uncomfortable reality of who they had become.

As they neared their destination, Charlotte excused herself to freshen up. In the cramped airplane restroom, she splashed her face with cold water and gazed at her reflection. Something had shifted within her. Maybe it was the joy of seeing Adam, but beneath that, a familiar unease lingered.

Why was her desire for him so deeply entwined with pain? The answer seemed clear, tied to the betrayal that had shattered their relationship. Yet now, faced with him again, she questioned whether it was her longing itself that perpetuated her suffering. Could her desire be the root of the pain she couldn't shake?

Psychologically, Charlotte recognized how desire often brings suffering. Desire, after all, highlights the gap between what is and what we yearn for, creating a sense of lack. Schopenhauer's philosophy echoed in her mind—desire inherently involves suffering because it's a striving for something unattainable or fleeting. Freud's ideas on unfulfilled desires manifesting as neuroses also resonated, making her wonder if this unresolved longing was keeping her trapped in a cycle of pain. Was her yearning for Adam really about him, or was it a projection of deeper unmet needs? If she could redefine her desire, shifting it away from him and toward self-fulfillment, could she begin to alleviate the pain?

As Charlotte returned to her seat, she realized Adam's presence in her life wasn't the work of fate but his own deliberate choice, perhaps driven by obsession. The bond they once shared was still there, but now it was laced with the clarity of someone who understood that love, when entwined with unresolved desire and past pain, might not be the answer she once believed it to be.

Why Does Desire Often Lead to Suffering?

It could be argued that humans consistently strive to evade pain and pursue pleasure, and much of human endeavor and decision-making stem from this tendency. Sigmund Freud posited that we inherently adhere to the pleasure principle from birth, seeking instant gratification of our desires. Fulfilling these desires elicits a profound sense of satisfaction from both our mind and our body. Conversely, the failure to meet these needs triggers an equally intense sensation of pain.

Freud suggests that personal development aims to shift from the pleasure principle to the reality principle, embracing delayed gratification. However, observations of human behavior indicate that many of us persist in operating within the pleasure principle even in later stages of life. In essence, transitioning to the reality principle signifies personal growth, a milestone not easily attained. While the pleasure principle offers immediate satisfaction, unmet desires can also cause significant distress. Recognizing this duality can alter our understanding of pain.

Freud's psychoanalytic theory is used to examine the complex interaction between the pleasure principle and the reality principle.[3] The pleasure principle, an inherent driving force, compels individuals to seek immediate gratification while avoiding discomfort. This primal instinct, deeply ingrained since birth, guides human behavior toward the pursuit of pleasure

---

3 Sigmund Freud, "Formulations Regarding the Two Principles in Mental Functioning," in *The Standard Edition of the Complete Psychological Works of Sigmund Freud*, ed. James Strachey (Hogarth Press, 1958).

and the avoidance of pain. In contrast, the reality principle signifies a developmental milestone where individuals adjust to the demands of the external world, acknowledging that not all desires can be instantly fulfilled. This transition entails weighing consequences, delaying gratification, and navigating reality's intricacies with rationality and moderation. *Pleasure and Reality* explores the nuanced dynamics between these principles, illuminating their impact on human behavior, personal growth, and therapeutic practices, providing valuable insights into the complexities of the human psyche.

Arthur Schopenhauer, the German philosopher, examines the pleasure principle through the lens of desire in his influential work *The World as Will and Representation.*[4] He suggests that humans perpetually fluctuate between desire and its fulfillment, both of which inherently entail suffering. Desire embodies unmet needs, breeding a sense of inadequacy that is inherently painful. Conversely, wish fulfillment often leads to feelings of emptiness and ennui, which also carry emotional distress. Schopenhauer posits that pain is therefore an unavoidable aspect of the human condition, and embracing this reality is central to the principle of acceptance.

If pain is an inherent facet of human existence, why do humans exhibit such an aversion to it? To address this query, we must examine the interplay between gain and loss. In business paradigms, a company's prosperity hinges on showcasing more profit

---

4 Arthur Schopenhauer, *The World as Will and Representation*, translated by E. F. J. Payne (Dover Publications, 1969).

than loss. However, no enterprise can thrive without encountering some measure of loss. Nonetheless, the greater the profit, the more esteemed the business. Life operates under a similar framework. Each day, we navigate decisions that entail forfeiting certain opportunities while gaining others. Those who make more calculated decisions often tend to achieve greater success. Nevertheless, human experience reveals that no one can consistently make flawless decisions, given the myriad unforeseen variables influencing outcomes, rendering complete foresight unattainable. Similar to the business domain, life planning entails a subjective evaluation of the profit/loss ratio, impacting our outcomes and consequently influencing our level of satisfaction to some extent.

When we perceive that our level of satisfaction outweighs our experience of pain, we often consider ourselves fortunate or successful. Conversely, if pain outweighs pleasure, feelings of dissatisfaction arise. By recognizing that some degree of pain is inevitable and accepting the losses inherent in life, similar to how businesses operate, we can learn to appreciate life's profits without becoming overwhelmed by the losses. However, many of us operate from a sense of entitlement that leaves no room for disappointment, leading us to adopt a victimized mindset and lament the perceived unfairness of life.

Finding Meaning amid Despair

In moments of despair, the process of meaning-making emerges as a beacon of hope. Meaning-making entails reevaluating one's perspective on life and its occurrences. Those with the capacity to sustain an integrated mindset can derive significance from both favorable and adverse experiences woven into their personal narrative. Victor Frankl, renowned for his work *Man's Search for Meaning*, posited that life isn't merely imposed upon us; instead, we actively shape our existence, and it falls upon us to uncover meaning in each moment, irrespective of circumstances.[5]

Victor Frankl's concept of meaning-making, rooted in existential psychology and logotherapy, offers a profound psychological perspective on human existence. Through his experiences in Nazi concentration camps, Frankl observed that even in the most dire circumstances, we have the capacity to find meaning and purpose in our lives. Central to Frankl's approach is the belief that humans possess the freedom to choose their attitudes and responses to life's challenges. He emphasized the importance of personal responsibility in the meaning-making process, highlighting that we each have the power to shape our own destiny. According to Frankl, meaning can be found through meaningful work, experiences of love and connection with others, and even in suffering. In essence, Frankl's psychological perspective on meaning-making underscores the inherent human capacity to find purpose and significance in every moment.

Achieving a delicate equilibrium between pleasure and pain demands a nuanced approach that intertwines mindfulness, self-awareness, and purposeful action. It begins with a deep-seated understanding of our values and priorities, allowing for the discernment of when momentary pleasures may lead to enduring distress

5 Viktor Frankl, *Man's Search for Meaning* (Beacon Press, 2006).

or when enduring temporary discomfort may pave the way for profound growth and fulfillment. Setting clear boundaries becomes paramount, enabling us to navigate the allure of immediate gratification while safeguarding against potential harm. Moreover, the cultivation of resilience through adversity fosters the capacity to withstand pain while extracting valuable lessons and insights.

This journey toward balance necessitates self-regulation, delaying gratification for greater rewards, and the pursuit of activities imbued with meaning and purpose. Seeking professional guidance, when needed, offers a structured pathway to integrate these strategies effectively, fostering a harmonious interplay between pleasure and pain in the pursuit of holistic well-being and fulfillment.

Reframing Pain and Desire in Relationships

In relationships, pain can often feel overwhelming, but it can also be a powerful catalyst for growth. For example, imagine going through a rough patch with your partner due to communication issues. Instead of seeing this as a negative experience, you could use it as an opportunity to learn more about each other's needs and communication styles. By addressing these issues constructively, the relationship can grow stronger, leading to deeper mutual understanding and respect.

Delaying immediate gratification can be crucial in relationships. For instance, if you're tempted to vent your frustrations in the heat of an argument, consider taking a moment to cool down and reflect instead. This pause can help you communicate more effectively later, prioritizing the long-term health of the relationship over the short-term release of anger. By focusing on constructive conversation, you work toward a more fulfilling and resilient partnership.

Building resilience in relationships is essential for navigating challenges together. For example, if you and your partner are facing financial stress, rather than letting it strain your relationship, you could develop a strategy together—such as budgeting or financial planning. Tackling the problem as a team not only helps to solve the issue but also strengthens your bond, making the relationship more resilient in the face of future challenges.

Patience and discipline are key in relationships, especially when dealing with recurring issues. Suppose you're working on improving trust after a breach. Instead of demanding immediate results, both partners can commit to consistent, small actions that rebuild trust over time, such as regular check-ins or transparent communication. This disciplined approach reinforces the commitment to healing and strengthens the foundation of the relationship.

Self-awareness in relationships involves recognizing the difference between fleeting desires and what truly fulfills you. For instance, after a disagreement, you might feel the urge to withdraw or seek comfort elsewhere. However, by reflecting on what truly matters—such as the long-term health of the relationship—you can choose actions that support genuine connection and fulfillment, like initiating an honest conversation or expressing vulnerability.

In relationships, embracing delayed gratification can involve focusing on long-term goals rather than immediate satisfaction. For example, if you and your partner are working toward a significant life goal, such as buying a home or starting a family, it might mean making sacrifices now—like cutting back on leisure spending or postponing vacations—to achieve that dream. This mindset shift fosters a deeper sense of shared purpose and strengthens the relationship over time.

Staying true to your relationship's long-term vision despite external pressures requires strong mutual understanding and shared values. For example, if societal or familial expectations are pressuring you to take certain steps—like getting married or having children before you're ready—you and your partner might choose to focus on what's right for you both instead. By setting boundaries and communicating openly, you can navigate these pressures together, ensuring that your relationship develops on your terms.

13

Integration Versus Disintegration

Charlotte sank onto the plush bed, gratefully kicking off her shoes upon entering the hotel. The midday journey from the airport, plagued by heavy traffic, had drained her. Although Adam had offered his driver, she preferred the anonymity and simplicity of a taxi ride. Checking the time, she noted her upcoming rendezvous with her sister for drinks. However, her weariness made her somewhat apathetic toward the impending plans.

Reclining on the bed, Charlotte found herself reflecting on the events of the past twenty-four hours with incredulity. It was almost surreal to think she had spent so much time in Adam's company, experiencing that familiar and undeniable connection once again. But among the warmth of their reunion, her doubts remained. Trusting him again felt like an insurmountable hurdle, rendering their relationship unlikely. Although he had orchestrated their reunion on the flight, ostensibly so they could speak, they hadn't discussed reconciliation. Struggling to maintain a sense of clarity, Charlotte attempted to push aside thoughts of him—to compartmentalize the emotional fallout from their encounter. But their shared past lingered, stirring within her a profound sense of longing and uncertainty that made detachment an uphill battle.

The piercing wail of sirens shattered the silence, jolting her back to the present moment. The sound seemed unnervingly close, echoing with an intensity that made her heart race. It reminded her of the chaos of that car accident many years ago, a memory she had desperately tried to suppress.

She was again transported back to that pivotal moment. The blaring sirens of the ambulance reverberated around her, drowning out all other sounds. She felt the warm blood trickling down her face, obscuring her vision and plunging her into a disorienting darkness. Shock immobilized her. Time seemed to stretch into infinity as she waited for help, each moment fraught with uncertainty and dread. Despite feeling everything acutely, the events unfolded before her like a surreal haze, leaving her profoundly disconnected from reality.

Her recollections carried her to the hospital, where she was shuttled from one sterile room to another, subjected to a battery of scans, MRIs, and earnest discussions among a rotating cast of doctors about her condition and the potential paths of treatment. In a pivotal moment, the lead surgeon approached her, his expression grave as he delicately broached the extent of her injuries. With measured words, he explained the grim reality: She had suffered a substantial loss of tissue on her face, the severity of damage to her left eye remaining uncertain. They proposed immediate surgery. His words hung heavy in the air, casting uncertainty over her already fragile state.

In a gesture both clinical and compassionate, the surgeon offered her a choice. If aesthetics were important to her, she could request a plastic surgeon. The idea that she was disfigured terrified her, and she asked to see herself. Despite his initial reluctance, he passed her a mirror. With trembling hands, she braced herself.

Her heart plummeted. Her left eye was sealed shut by swollen flesh. Skin hung loosely from her forehead and the left side of her head. The image bore little resemblance to the face she had known. It was a stark reminder of the fragility of life and the arbitrary cruelty of fate. But amid the devastation, she felt a flicker of gratitude. Her right eye remained intact, a small mercy amid the overwhelming despair.

Setting the mirror aside, Charlotte resolved to take control of her circumstances. She reached for her phone and began making calls to ensure she received the specialized care and support she needed. She was determined to reclaim her life in the wake of tragedy, and she found solace in her resilience. A natural crisis manager, Charlotte found herself confronted with a challenge of unparalleled proportions. It was, without a doubt, the most difficult trial she had ever faced—until an even greater injury.

Turning to the treating surgeon, she mustered the courage to voice her fears. "Can you please provide me with an update on my father? They transported him to a different hospital."

The doctor's gaze fell to the floor. "I'm deeply sorry," he said. "Your father didn't survive."

In an instant, a new realm of anguish engulfed Charlotte, eclipsing the pain she had already been grappling with. It was a gut-wrenching blow that shattered her world, leaving her adrift in a sea of unfathomable grief. From that moment forward, the weight of loss bore down on her with a ferocity that surpassed anything she had ever known, casting a shadow over her very existence.

As the doctor's lips continued to move, the world muted itself, leaving Charlotte alone with the overwhelming weight of her grief. Primal anguish consumed her, causing her to scream like a wounded animal. Her body convulsed with desperation, as if seeking to escape the unbearable reality. A few nurses rushed to her side, their gentle hands attempting to restrain her. One of the nurses administered a sedative. The sharp prick of the needle pierced the haze of despair that had enveloped Charlotte. As the medication took effect, the edges of her consciousness began to blur, the world around her fading.

Now, lying in her hotel bed and listening to the street outside, the cacophony of sirens dulled to a distant hum, the echoes of her anguish receding into memory. Although the harrowing ordeal of that accident had occurred long ago, the specter lingered in her mind all these years later, a reminder of the sorrow she had once endured.

Despite her best efforts to silence the clamor of her thoughts, Charlotte found herself ensnared in the tumult of her emotions, each attempt to distance herself only serving to entangle her further. Frustration welled up, a seething resentment toward the vulnerability that threatened to overwhelm her carefully cultivated composure. She loathed this sensation, the feeling of losing herself to the tempest within. The poised facade of adulthood was slipping away, leaving behind a wounded child desperate for solace in the fleeting comfort of instant gratification. No matter how fiercely she fought against it, the tide of emotion seemed insurmountable, dragging her down into fragmented despair.

This struggle was not unfamiliar to her; she had waged this battle before. But no matter how valiantly she fought, the wounded child within her always seemed to emerge victorious, leaving her adrift in misery for days on end until the steady hand of adulthood regained control once more.

In many ways, this lack of control mirrored the fragmented memories that haunted her from the day of the accident. They reminded her of the fragility of her psyche, a testament to the enduring power of unresolved trauma to wreak havoc on her fragile sense of self.

Her mind turned back to that instant gratification: Adam. The thought of waiting for him to make a move turned Charlotte's stomach. How had he managed to unravel her hard-won emotional stability with just a simple conversation? She despised her vulnerability around him, yearning to remain indifferent. She tried to maintain a facade of stoic composure, but her emotions in his presence seemed to betray her, revealing a desperation she abhorred. It was infuriating how all her inner strength seemed to evaporate in his presence, leaving her at his mercy. Her sense of self-worth had become irrevocably entwined with his actions; that realization left her feeling hollow and diminished. How could she allow someone else's validation—or lack thereof—to dictate her own value?

Clutching the pillow tightly to her chest, Charlotte stifled her cries, feeling the weight of her own self-recrimination pressing down upon her. With a deep breath, she released the pent-up frustration and disappointment, allowing the scream to escape her lips to expel the negativity.

In that moment of release, she reclaimed her sense of agency, determined not to let her self-worth be dictated by external validation. She knew that, even in her darkest moments, she was worthy of love and respect, regardless of whether it came from Adam, from someone else, or even from within herself. With each breath, she felt the chaotic storm within her begin to subside, allowing the cool waters of logic to once again course through her veins.

Leaning back against the pillows, she cast a gentle gaze inward, allowing herself to confront the wounded child within. In the past, she might have viewed this vulnerable aspect of herself with disdain, condemning her perceived weakness as a failure of character. But in this moment of raw vulnerability, she discovered a new compassion for her wounded soul. With empathy in her heart, Charlotte recognized the profound yearning for love and security that had driven her to fixate on Adam. Rather than judgment, she felt a swell of compassion for this hurting part of herself, understanding the depth of her pain and longing for comfort amid the turmoil.

Charlotte allowed herself to fully embrace her grief, shedding tears for the agony she recognized within the wounded child. In this moment of vulnerability, she found solace in the simple act of acknowledging and honoring her pain, a small yet significant step toward healing and self-compassion.

In the gentle embrace of empathy and stillness, Charlotte experienced a profound shift in perspective that bestowed a renewed sense of agency and control over her circumstances. With this shift came a welcome wave of peace and ease.

Charlotte found solace in the knowledge that she held the power to navigate her own emotional landscape, even in the face of uncertainty and heartache. Although the path forward may be fraught with challenges, she took comfort in the quiet strength she discovered within herself—a strength born not from the absence of pain but from the courage to confront it with grace. She found herself able to detach from her pain, stepping back to observe it. This shift allowed her to perceive Adam not through the lens of idealization she had constructed in her mind but as the flawed and multifaceted individual he truly was.

From this vantage point, she could see him in his entirety—the strengths and virtues that had initially drawn her to him, as well as the imperfections and shortcomings that had become increasingly apparent over time. As the romanticized veil fell away, she found herself liberated from the confines of intense infatuation, her emotions no longer tethered to the illusion of perfection she had projected onto him. Adam ceased to be an omnipotent figure of adoration and became a mortal being, replete with both commendable attributes and inherent flaws. The prospect of losing him no longer seemed as devastating, no longer an insurmountable obstacle to her happiness; rather, it was an unfortunate circumstance that could be navigated and eventually transcended. She embraced the freedom to release her attachment to the idealized version of Adam, allowing herself to move forward with a sense of grace and resilience. In this space of acceptance and understanding, she found the strength to forge a path forward, unencumbered by the weight of unrealistic expectations and unattainable fantasies.

Over the years, Charlotte had carved out a space in her heart exclusively for the idealized version of Adam, the embodiment of her romanticized fantasies. As she gained deeper insight into herself and her relationships, she found herself gradually shifting toward a more grounded and realistic perception of him, stripped of the veil of infatuation.

In moments of clarity, she longed to bottle this perspective up, to draw from its wisdom whenever her less refined emotions threatened to overwhelm her. But she understood that the journey toward integration was a process that required patience, self-compassion, and an unwavering commitment to growth.

Acknowledging the coexistence of her fragmented and intact selves, Charlotte embraced the complexity of her inner landscape. She recognized that, while the idealized version of Adam held sway over her heart, the fragmented aspects of herself still clamored for acknowledgment and understanding. With each passing day, she made space for both sides within herself, allowing room for the intricate interplay of light and shadow. Although the broken parts of herself might occasionally take control, she knew that they would pass, paving the way for a deeper sense of integration and self-awareness.

Armed with this wisdom, Charlotte recommenced her journey with renewed determination, embracing the full spectrum of her being with an open heart and a steadfast resolve to continue growing, evolving, and embracing the beauty of her inherent complexity.

As Charlotte gazed out the window, she noticed that the sun had already dipped below the horizon; she had been lost in her thoughts for hours. Despite the passage of time, an unexpected lightness enveloped her. With a surge of energy, she propelled herself out of bed. She headed straight for the shower and allowed the warm water to cascade over her, washing away the emotional turmoil that had weighed her down for so long. In its place, a sense of renewal blossomed within her—a sudden desire to venture out into the world, to embrace life with a fervor that had long lain dormant. With each passing moment, her excitement swelled. The prospect of reconnecting with the vibrant, adventurous part of herself that had been overshadowed by the pain of Adam was exhilarating.

Sorting through her suitcase, Charlotte's fingertips grazed the delicate lace of a black dress, its intricate patterns immediately captivating her attention. She took a moment to appreciate its allure. Despite the challenge of fastening the zipper, she embraced the task as an opportunity to conquer something with ease.

With the dress clinging to her curves in all the right places, Charlotte felt a surge of confidence wash over her. Pausing for a moment to admire her reflection in the mirror, she reached for a pair of stunning sandals, their elegant design accentuating the length of her legs. As she dressed, Charlotte felt anticipation building within her. With each movement, she felt her past burdens begin to lift, replaced by a freedom and possibility.

Whispering to herself with a grin, she declared, "London, here I come."

How Can You Find Wholeness amid Fragmentation?

Integration is the act of harmoniously coordinating various elements into a unified whole, while disintegration involves the breakdown and decomposition of those elements. When things come together in a cohesive manner, a sense of peace and unity emerges, leading to integration. Conversely, when things start to fall apart and lose their coherence, a feeling of disunity arises, representing disintegration. We thrive when we are in a state of integration, both within ourselves and in our external environment.

From a developmental perspective, integration and disintegration are often observed during periods of transition and growth, such as adolescence or midlife crises. These phases can be characterized by intense inner turmoil as we grapple with conflicting emotions, values, and identities. Successful navigation through these stages typically involves a process of integration, where we gradually reconcile and integrate different aspects of ourselves into a more unified identity. Overall, integration and disintegration represent fundamental processes in psychological development, reflecting the ongoing quest for coherence, authenticity, and wholeness within the individual psyche.

If we examine this concept in relation to distress, we can observe a positive correlation between stress and disintegration. The more confusion and pressure we experience, the more likely we are to navigate toward a fragmented state. As we regain control over a situation, tension decreases, and a sense of consolidation emerges, guiding us toward integration.

Similar to how stress manifests as tension in the body, leading to soreness and tightness in muscles, it can also induce rigidity in our thoughts and emotions. This rigidity limits our ability to perceive situations beyond pain and suffering. People in this state often describe feeling trapped in a cycle of misery, yearning to break free. Disintegration sets in, making it increasingly difficult to shift perspectives and adopt a more creative mindset. It becomes a challenging journey through a dark labyrinth of pain.

For change to occur, our thoughts and emotions must regain flexibility, enabling us to explore alternative options. This fluidity gives rise to a state of creativity, empowering us to reorganize our understanding of the information at hand. This transformative process is known as integration. In this state, we possess the capacity to adapt to our environment and circumstances rather than feeling victimized and immobilized. We can navigate through the chaos with resilience and openness, embracing growth and transformation.

Within each of us are multiple personality traits that may sometimes be at odds with one another. For instance, you might want the security of a committed relationship while also craving personal freedom. This lack of harmony between your needs and desires can lead to a sense of fragmentation, pulling you in different directions and causing inconsistency, a lack of persistence, and inflexibility. To restore a state of integration, it is essential to attempt to harmonize these conflicting reactions into a unified whole.

This unification typically occurs when the less dominant traits gradually integrate with the more dominant ones. Expanding on the previous example, if you are in a developmental stage where the desire for commitment aligns with your core needs but you are not yet ready to relinquish your freedom, the need for fidelity and connection becomes the core personality trait, and the desire for freedom becomes the less dominant trait. Integration in this scenario involves a gradual negotiation with the less dominant trait, leading to a shift toward a state that is in harmony with commitment. As this shift occurs, the internal duality begins to oscillate toward conformity.

Imagine an individual who places a high value on intellectual exploration and autonomy, yet finds themselves in a deeply fulfilling romantic relationship. Initially, they may feel a tension between their intellectual pursuits, which demand solitude and freedom, and the intimacy and fidelity that their relationship requires. Over time, however, this person may begin to experience a shift in their priorities, gradually integrating their need for independence with a commitment to their partner.

This integration doesn't mean forsaking intellectual pursuits; rather, it involves a nuanced negotiation, where the person learns to honor their autonomy while embracing the stability and depth that commitment provides. As this shift unfolds, the internal duality between freedom and fidelity begins to balance, allowing for a harmonious state where both desires coexist in a refined and balanced way.

In the journey of personal transformation, it's crucial to recognize that change is a gradual process, often unfolding in stages and requiring us to make sacrifices along the way. It's important to delve into our desires, carefully observing the inner workings of our minds and hearts. After each trial, it's essential to reflect on our progress and reevaluate our path forward.

Through repeated attempts and self-reflection, we eventually reach a point where we must make definitive choices. However, it's vital to understand that this process can be lengthy, and the tension between conflicting desires may persist for an extended period. As we navigate through these challenges, it's imperative to exercise patience and compassion toward ourselves. Remember, personal growth is a journey, and each step forward, no matter how small, brings us closer to our goals.

Moving Toward a More Integrated Self

In relationships, unconscious beliefs or patterns often influence interactions. For example, someone might realize they have a pattern of choosing partners who are emotionally distant, which could stem from childhood experiences with an unavailable parent. By recognizing this pattern, they can consciously seek out relationships with partners who are more emotionally available, thereby breaking the cycle and fostering healthier connections.

Inner conflicts are common in relationships, such as feeling torn between wanting closeness and fearing vulnerability. For instance, a person might desire deep emotional intimacy with their partner but also fear getting hurt, leading to a push-pull dynamic. By identifying and reconciling these conflicting desires, perhaps through open communication or therapy, the couple can work toward a more balanced and satisfying relationship.

Spirituality or existential questioning can deepen the meaning within relationships. For example, a couple might explore how their shared spiritual beliefs influence their relationship's purpose. They could engage in practices like meditating together or discussing existential topics, which might help them integrate these insights into a more profound and purpose-driven connection.

Acknowledging and integrating difficult aspects of oneself, often referred to as shadow work, is crucial for relational growth. For instance, someone might realize they have been projecting their insecurities onto their partner, leading to unnecessary conflicts. By bringing these shadow aspects into awareness—perhaps through self-reflection or couples counseling—they can address these issues, leading to a healthier and more authentic relationship.

Unresolved traumas can significantly impact current relationships. A person who experienced betrayal in a past relationship might struggle with trust in their current relationship. Engaging in healing processes, such as therapy or support groups, can help them address these traumas and integrate the experiences, allowing them to build trust and security in their current relationship.

Cultivating a sense of interconnectedness with others and the world around you can enhance relational bonds. For instance, a couple might decide to volunteer together in their community. This shared experience can help them feel more connected not only to each other but also to a broader social network, fostering empathy and a deeper understanding of collective experiences.

Creative or expressive outlets can be powerful tools for relational integration. For example, a couple might take up a shared hobby, like dancing or painting, which allows them to express emotions and experiences in a nonverbal way. This shared activity can deepen their bond and help them process complex feelings, leading to greater understanding and connection within the relationship.

14

Love Versus Infatuation

Charlotte stood in line at the coat check, waiting to retrieve her coat before stepping out into the cold London night. It was her third evening abroad, filled with good food, laughter, and the company of friends. She had met with her sister a few times during her stay, but every conversation had veered dangerously close to Adam. Charlotte, not ready to confront that fragile subject, had steered things away each time. After a long day of lectures and socializing, she was more than ready to leave it all behind and call it a night.

As each minute passed, Charlotte grew increasingly impatient. The wine had left her with a lingering headache, and all she wanted was to return to her room and sleep. The young woman at the coat check apologetically handed her a man's coat, questioning whether she had the correct number. Irritated, Charlotte sarcastically replied with a raised voice and rolled eyes. "No, I must have picked up someone else's ticket." She immediately regretted her words, realizing their harshness.

To her surprise, a tall, serious-looking man approached her with her coat. He held it out for her and mentioned that their numbers must have been mixed up. Charlotte politely returned his coat and thanked him for his kindness. He held the door open for her and tipped the girl at the stand before following Charlotte outside. The stranger seemed to recognize her embarrassment and commented, "It's a busy night. She's doing her best."

Charlotte nodded in acknowledgment.

The man asked whether Charlotte had transportation for the evening. She explained that a car from the hotel was scheduled to pick her up. After exchanging polite goodbyes, Charlotte hurried toward her car. In her haste, her heel got caught in a crack in the pavement, nearly causing her to trip.

Still nearby, the stranger came to her aid. He offered his arm for support, and Charlotte gratefully accepted. He asked if she was okay and assisted in untangling her heel from the pavement. Charlotte smiled appreciatively and jokingly remarked, "You're turning into quite the rescuer tonight. I hope this doesn't become a trend."

The man smiled. "Happy to help." Extending his hand for a handshake, he introduced himself as Tarek.

Charlotte reciprocated the gesture, feeling grateful for the unexpected assistance. Tarek commented on how cold Charlotte's hand was and suggested a warm beverage. Charlotte was about to politely decline when she recalled Tarek's gentlemanly behavior and decided to accept. He placed his hand on her back and guided her toward a charming coffee house at the corner of the street. The place appeared empty and quiet, and a cozy fireplace at the far end immediately drew Charlotte toward it. Tarek followed and pulled out a chair for her.

Suddenly, Charlotte remembered the car waiting for her and excused herself to call the service to inform them of her delay. When she returned, she found two warm beverages and some desserts on the table. Impressed, she sat down, took a bite of a cookie, and discovered it tasted heavenly. She praised his choice, and the next hour passed as they engaged in casual conversation, getting to know each other. Charlotte learned that Tarek was three years her senior, was divorced, and had an investment company near her hometown of Los Angeles back in the US. Like Charlotte, he was in London for a mix of business and pleasure. While he seemed like a nice, stable guy, Charlotte found him somewhat dull and lacking any sense of magic. She noticed herself passing judgment on him and immediately disliked her attitude.

The next hour passed pleasantly, and they exchanged contact information before bidding each other farewell. Charlotte hurriedly got into the warm car, intrigued by this stranger whose presence, while not inherently captivating, strangely brought her a sense of calm. There was nothing particularly striking about him—solid, safe, and lacking in allure—but his composed demeanor embodied stability and predictability. This contrasted sharply with the chaos and unpredictability she often found herself drawn to. He represented a life of safety and security, prompting her to ponder what it might be like to be with someone who didn't bring about turmoil and uncertainty.

However, as she mulled over these thoughts, she came to the realization that an attraction to problems and the thrill of playing with fire were deeply ingrained in her. Changing her nature would not be a simple task. She found pleasure in the challenge, the excitement, and the adrenaline rush that accompanied a life of uncertainty. It was as if she was addicted to that uncertainty, despite being aware that playing with fire carried the risk of getting burned.

She was torn between the stability and safety offered by someone like Tarek and the allure of the risky and unpredictable relationship like the one she had with Adam. She understood that at some point, she would need to make a decision; but for the time being, the excitement of the unknown continued to beckon her. Ironically, she was acutely aware of the price she paid for the thrill of unpredictability. And if she were to be honest with herself, she'd have to admit the thrill was starting to feel costly.

The following day was filled with more meetings. Charlotte had not heard from Adam since they saw each other on the plane. Despite her best efforts, thoughts of him continuously occupied her mind, and she would be lying to herself if she didn't admit how impatiently she waited for him to reach out.

It was a rare sunny day in London, making the city enticing for exploration. Charlotte decided to go to Chelsea and stroll around before meeting her friend for tea. She had barely taken a few steps when she glanced down at her phone and noticed a message from Adam. His number was no longer saved, but she recognized it. Her heart sank, and she stood frozen for a few minutes, annoying a couple of people who bumped into her on the street. Startled by their reactions, she moved to a quieter spot and opened the text.

The message read, *Hey, how is your trip going?*

Simple and neutral, but it sent shivers down her spine. All she knew was that he still cared enough to ask. She decided to cool down her excitement by grabbing an ice cream. She ordered a caramel cone from the confused-looking guy behind the counter and walked outside, feeling the sun on her skin.

After devouring the ice cream, she picked up her phone and simply replied, *Marvelously.*

Adam immediately responded, *Well, why don't we discuss it over steak tonight? I have a table reserved for us at 7.*

Charlotte wanted to accept, but she couldn't bring herself to immediately say yes. Summoning her courage, she wrote, *Sorry, it would have to be a table for one. I already have dinner plans.*

Charlotte knew how much Adam hated rejection, so she assumed that would be the last she heard from him. However, a part of her desperately wanted to see how much he was willing to chase her.

To her surprise, he replied, *Would it be presumptuous of me to change the reservation to tomorrow night?*

She read the message and held the phone close to her heart. Somehow this man still made her feel butterflies in her stomach.

Her image of him—idealized, she knew—took her to a magical place where everything seemed wonderful, and his absence felt like an unpleasant fall back into reality. She couldn't stop smiling; there he was again, wanting her back. It wasn't supposed to be like this anymore. She thought she had overcome it, realizing that he wasn't as significant as she once believed—that her feelings for him were just the result of the trauma she carried. But healing wasn't that simple. It came in layers, slowly, and just when she thought she was free, she'd find herself pulled back in. That constant pull, the cycle of thinking she was done only to be reminded she wasn't, was exhausting.

She replied, *Not presumptuous, just optimistic.*

The next evening, Adam arrived at her hotel half an hour before she expected him and called to see if she was ready to grab a drink before dinner. Charlotte had already decided that one drink would suffice for the evening. She wanted to keep her wits about her, so she politely excused herself, informing him that she would come down in time for dinner.

As Charlotte walked into the bar, his gaze landed on her. There was a mesmerized look in his eyes that she adored. When they were together, he often looked at her like this when she entered a room, his eyes brimming with fondness and adoration. She returned his affectionate gaze with a smile, prompting him to extend his hand toward her, and she took it.

He held her at a distance for a moment and looked her up and down, admiring her dress. He murmured, "There is nothing I like more than a woman who can pull off a white winter look."

Leaning forward, he gave her a kiss on the cheek, causing her heart to pound. He offered her a seat at the bar and suggested, "We should probably leave soon to get there on time, but we have time for a quick drink."

Charlotte thanked him for the offer but again refused, heading for the door. For a moment, she had forgotten all that he had put her through. All she wanted was to be with him again, and the thought of that scared her beyond belief. He had cast a spell on her. Part of her wanted to run away, but the enchantment was too strong, so she stayed put, awaiting her fate.

Is It True Love or Infatuation?

Often, what people perceive as falling in love is simply a state of infatuation, intense emotions of admiration toward another person. Infatuation is characterized by fascination and fixation. The term *falling in love* is a fitting metaphor for infatuation, because it implies a lack of intention and is merely a result of chance.

According to Helen Fisher, the concept of love revolves around three primary brain systems: lust, attraction, and attachment.[6] Lust involves the primal drive of sexual desire, fueled by hormones like testosterone and estrogen. Attraction encompasses intense feelings of romantic passion and infatuation, driven by neurotransmitters such as dopamine, norepinephrine, and

6 Helen Fisher, *Anatomy of Love: A Natural History of Mating, Marriage, and Why We Stray.* (W.W. Norton & Company, 2016)

serotonin. Attachment involves deep emotional bonding and long-term commitment, facilitated by hormones like oxytocin and vasopressin. Together, these three systems work in tandem to create the multifaceted experience of romantic love, encompassing both the initial stages of infatuation and the enduring bonds between partners.

According to Fisher's model of love, infatuation is associated with the attraction stage. This stage is characterized by intense feelings of romantic passion, obsession, and longing for another person. Dopamine, norepinephrine, and serotonin create a euphoric and exhilarating experience often described as love. Infatuation typically occurs in the early stages of a romantic relationship, when the individuals are deeply attracted to each other and experience intense emotional and physical desire. According to Fisher, true love is marked by a balance between the excitement and intensity of attraction and the stability and security of attachment, creating a fulfilling and lasting bond between individuals.

Love involves an element of decision-making, which can only occur when there is sufficient knowledge and evidence of compatibility and sustainability. Regrettably, we frequently misinterpret the intense euphoria of infatuation as love, rather than acknowledging it as the chemical high that it truly is.

To differentiate between love and infatuation, we can argue that love is a deep feeling of connection that has withstood the test of reality, whereas infatuation is a superficial connection rooted in a fantasy of attraction. Love usually develops over time through connection and positive reinforcement; it is a byproduct of knowing and choosing. Fascination, on the other hand, is a quick physiological response based on imagination and projection. In love, we truly see a person for who they are and decide to love them in their entirety, flaws included. In infatuation, we create an idealized version of the other person and love the fantasy rather than the truth.

Love is other-centered: We genuinely see someone for who they are in order to develop feelings of love. It is based on genuine bonding and enduring closeness. In love, we understand and accept imperfections, and we willingly compromise and sacrifice to maintain intimacy. Infatuation, on the other hand, is self-centered, as we love what we want the other person to be rather than who they truly are. When infatuated, our main concern is how wonderful the other person makes us feel, and as soon as we realize that this feeling is not everlasting, we feel the need to break away.

Love necessitates understanding, attentiveness, and introspection. Our capacity to love another is contingent upon our self-awareness and our ability to genuinely comprehend them and ourselves. In contrast, infatuation often lacks these essential elements. If we were truly self-aware, we would recognize and address our own needs rather than projecting them onto others for fulfillment.

Love and infatuation are not mutually exclusive, however. In fact, it can be argued that infatuation can evolve into love with compatibility and knowledge. In other words, most if not all love affairs begin with a spark of infatuation, but not all infatuations transform into love. After the initial attraction, a person can lose interest if the other person fails to live up to their fantasy or if the attraction is not mutual. The key to turning infatuation into love lies in the willingness to tolerate disappointment. If both individuals show the ability to consistently compromise and sacrifice despite disappointments, the result can be a mutual bond of respect and admiration.

Embracing Pain to Grow

The notion of tolerating disappointments or making sacrifices and compromises does not entail enduring situations that are detrimental to us or cause harm. Rather, it entails a willingness to embrace differences and withstand the discomfort that accompanies growth within the relationship. This underscores the significance of self-awareness. A healthy relational dynamic thrives when it enables us to stay authentic to ourselves and attend to our individual needs.

Sue Johnson, a prominent psychologist and researcher known for her work in couple's therapy and attachment theory, emphasizes the significance of emotional responsiveness and secure attachment in fostering true love.[7] According to Johnson, true love is characterized by a deep emotional bond between partners, rooted in a sense of safety, trust, and connection. In her approach, known as emotionally focused therapy, Johnson focuses on

7 Sue Johnson, *Hold Me Tight: Seven Conversations for a Lifetime of Love* (Little, Brown and Company, 2008).

helping couples cultivate greater emotional intimacy and responsiveness to each other's needs, ultimately strengthening their bond and fostering a more satisfying and enduring relationship. She believes that true love is nurtured through empathy, vulnerability, and mutual understanding, enabling partners to create a secure and supportive emotional connection that transcends challenges and difficulties.

This highlights the crucial role of safety and security within a relational dynamic. Because of the intense vulnerability inherent in relationships, the absence of this sense of safety leaves the couple exposed to raw emotional pain. Essentially, when we engage in a relational dynamic devoid of genuine care and security, we subject ourselves to potential suffering. While it's true that no relationship is ever completely risk-free and that life itself is unpredictable, we should at least feel a sense of safety and security in a romantic relationship in order to flourish. This illusion of safety provides a foundation for trust, emotional intimacy, and the cultivation of true love.

The question of why some people are drawn to more unpredictable patterns of love despite the universal human need for safety and security is complex. While safety and security are indeed fundamental needs for all humans, other factors can influence how we navigate our romantic relationships. These factors may include past experiences, learned behaviors, personality traits, and cultural influences. For example, people who have experienced trauma or insecure attachment in childhood may subconsciously replicate these patterns in their adult relationships, even if it means sacrificing safety and security. Additionally, societal norms and media portrayals of love and romance can shape people's perceptions and expectations, leading them to prioritize passion and excitement over stability and security. Ultimately, the interplay of various psychological, social, and environmental factors can contribute to why some individuals gravitate toward more unpredictable patterns of love, even when those patterns conflict with their inherent need for safety and security. Understanding these dynamics can be a crucial step in fostering healthier and more fulfilling relationships.

What Is Your Love Pattern?

Identifying negative love patterns within ourselves requires self-awareness, introspection, and a willingness to explore past experiences and current relationship dynamics. To help identify negative love patterns, start by reflecting on your past relationships: Are there any recurring themes or patterns? Pay attention to common behaviors, conflicts, and outcomes that may have occurred in multiple relationships. Next, examine your family dynamics: Consider how patterns of love and relationships were modeled in your family of origin. Reflect on the dynamics between your parents or caregivers, as well as your own experiences of love and attachment growing up.

Then recognize triggers and patterns: Pay attention to situations or circumstances that trigger certain emotions or behaviors in your relationships. Identify any patterns of communication, conflict resolution, or attachment styles that may be contributing to negative dynamics. You should also seek feedback from trusted individuals; sometimes, others may have insights into our behavior and patterns that we may not see ourselves. Consider seeking feedback from close friends, family members, or a therapist who can offer an outside perspective.

Consider your beliefs and values as well: Reflect on your beliefs and values about love, relationships, and yourself. Consider whether any negative beliefs or attitudes may be influencing your behavior and relationship patterns. Learn about different attachment styles, such as secure, anxious-preoccupied, dismissive-avoidant, or fearful-avoidant. Reflect on which attachment style may resonate with you and how it may impact your relationships. Finally, a journal can be a helpful tool for self-reflection and tracking patterns in your thoughts, feelings, and behaviors related to love and relationships. Don't just think about all of this; write it down. By engaging in these self-reflective practices, you can gain insight into your negative love patterns and take steps toward fostering healthier and more fulfilling relationships.

Deepening Relationships Through Genuine Connection

Moving from infatuation to love requires an emotional shift—one that fosters empathy, genuine care, and mutual understanding. The depth of emotional connection you build over time goes beyond fleeting passion. Consider ways to express empathy and care that reinforce your bond: active listening, supporting your partner's emotional needs, and recognizing their worth beyond the initial attraction. Think about a time when your partner was struggling emotionally, and instead of offering surface-level reassurances, you listened deeply, validating their feelings. That moment of empathy and emotional presence likely helped foster a deeper connection that transcends infatuation.

In this phase, the balance between excitement and stability becomes crucial. Spontaneous weekend getaways or surprise dates are great for keeping the excitement alive, but it's equally important to create routines or rituals that ground your relationship in stability, such as regular check-ins or shared hobbies that foster emotional security.

Managing expectations is key to fostering love. Where infatuation often creates an idealized version of the other, love demands acceptance of imperfections. Perhaps you've had moments where your partner's flaws—like their forgetfulness or need for alone time—clash with your expectations. Instead of allowing frustration to build, you worked on embracing these imperfections, realizing they're part of what makes your partner human and unique. This acceptance signals a deeper emotional investment.

To deepen your connection, be intentional about nurturing both physical and emotional intimacy. This involves more than grand gestures; it is about consistent, small acts of care that build trust and vulnerability over time. Regular, honest conversations that go beyond surface-level discussions can foster an emotional bond that grows stronger with time. For instance, setting aside time each week to talk openly about your feelings or dreams can create emotional closeness, while small gestures like leaving thoughtful notes or making time for physical affection help build a solid foundation of trust and intimacy. Sharing meaningful experiences, supporting one another's personal growth, and being present in moments of vulnerability will create a space where love can flourish.

Sustaining love requires a conscious effort to maintain self-awareness and mutual respect. Personal growth is not just an individual journey but a shared one. Reflect on a time when your partner took on a new challenge—whether it was starting a new job, pursuing a hobby, or making a major life change—and you supported them fully. Your willingness to encourage their personal development, while balancing your own growth, indicates a relationship that's moving beyond infatuation toward love that nurtures mutual success. Prioritizing the emotional and psychological well-being of both partners ensures that your relationship does not become stagnant but continues to evolve.

In this transition, the goal is to cultivate a love that is sustainable—one that withstands the inevitable challenges and joys of life, built on a foundation of trust, understanding, and a shared commitment to growth. By embracing this process, you move from the fleeting intensity of infatuation to the profound depth of lasting love.

15

Victim Versus Survivor

Charlotte couldn't suppress her smile; she was enchanted. Her time with Adam in London had been nothing short of magical, and she considered prolonging her stay. They savored afternoon tea, delved into the treasures of a museum, and even embraced the tranquility of canoeing on the Thames. Late-night indulgences in snacks and lively explorations of street food markets echoed the joy of their past days together in New York. It felt as though time had rewound, returning them to where they had begun. They spoke about everything—their aspirations, their loved ones, and their future prospects—but they quietly avoided speaking of their own relationship.

Seated on a bench within the tranquil confines of Saint Dunstan in the East, Charlotte discovered solace in her cherished hidden garden. She hugged her legs close, seeking warmth beneath the layers of her heavy jacket. Despite the briskness of the air, she reveled in the serenity of this medieval church, now a garden. Bearing witness to the remnants of its resilience amid the ravages of World War II, the surviving walls stood as a poignant reminder of endurance and the capacity to find beauty amid destruction.

Glancing at her watch, Charlotte realized she had whiled away over two hours lost in introspection, but she found herself reluctant to leave London—or, more accurately, to leave Adam. She knew their idyllic reverie could not endure. Responsibilities beckoned, as did the reality of their past. As she lingered, Charlotte realized that it wasn't London or Adam tethering her; it was the resurging vitality within her. She admitted to herself that, following the end of their relationship, she had been a mere shell of her former self. While she mechanically fulfilled her obligations, true happiness had eluded her.

The sensation of emptiness and stagnation resonated deeply with Charlotte, reminding her of the despair following her accident and the loss of her father. A fragment of her essence had perished in the accident, leaving her in a state of emotional paralysis and vacancy. Her once vibrant connection to herself and the world was profoundly transformed—until Adam's arrival.

The previous evening, Charlotte had attended a charity ball hosted by a close friend. Although she had invited Adam, she made it clear they needed to be discreet mingling with others throughout the event. Given the complexity of their past, she was determined not to allow their interactions to be misinterpreted. As such, she wasn't ready to answer any questions about the relationship or to entertain a potential reconciliation. She still grappled with the idea of letting him back into her life, uncertain if she could ever fully embrace it.

Throughout the evening, Adam intensely fixated on her every move, silently expressing his yearning. Despite her lack of interest in engaging with anyone else, she resisted his advances to uphold their agreement. After dinner, he ask her to dance. She hesitated, but upon his whispered reminder that "it's for charity," she relented, extending her hand to his.

As they danced, Adam guided Charlotte through the intricate steps of the tango, patiently correcting her when she lost count. His touch was reassuringly firm against the backless chiffon dress she wore, and his gaze held a longing that anchored her in the moment whenever she attempted to escape. At one point, he endeavored to lift her for a *calesita*, triggering a flood of memories from their initial encounter on the staircase. She recalled how he had charmed her with his moves and captivating presence, drawing her out of her pain. She had still been grappling with the profound loss of her father and her own injuries from the accident. The pain of her father's passing had been a burden she eventually learned to bear, but the ensuing turmoil within the family had proven to be the most challenging.

To Charlotte, Adam had once been a beacon in the dark, only to disappoint her profoundly. And now he had returned, tempting to rescue her from the ache of his absence. Like before, he was a refreshing breeze, and there was a part of her longing to be enveloped in his embrace and to forget the turmoil of the past. This part of her still hoped for that happily-ever-after.

But a resilient part of her had surfaced. This newfound strength grasped the truth that light and darkness coexisted and that she wielded the powers of responsibility and accountability. She had come to understand that she didn't rely on Adam or anyone else to effect the changes she sought. The choice to reclaim her happiness lay solely within her own hands.

In the depths of her despair, Charlotte felt adrift and forsaken. Her own grief was heavy enough, but she also carried the burden of consoling her mother and sisters, each grappling with their own pain and sorrow. With that memory overwhelming her, she abruptly excused herself from the dancefloor. Adam followed her to the terrace, where he discovered her gasping for air, clinging to the railing. Without uttering a word, he enveloped her in a comforting embrace, whispering reassurances. In that poignant moment, Charlotte found solace in the arms of this man who now felt like a stranger, briefly remembering her resolve not to allow him to rescue her from her pain so he could later inflict more.

Back in the ruins of the church garden, she contemplated whether she truly craved rescue anymore. The notion of being saved held a seductive allure, but she recognized it as a surrender of her own power, entrusting her happiness to someone. This time, she acknowledged that only she could rescue herself.

Brimming with potential and hope, she realized that the pivotal change lay in her independence from seeking validation and salvation from others. She had mastered the art of creating her own light by painstakingly assembling her shattered fragments, clawing her way out of the abyss. For anyone who has weathered loss, this act of self-rescue embodies true strength, an indomitable force that can never be erased.

Her conflicting desires and needs waged war within her, with neither emerging as the victor on that morning. One certainty remained: She could no longer delude herself with fairy tales. She saw Adam for his true essence—both his capacity for love and his propensity for disappointment. She couldn't deny that traces of her affection for him lingered, but she refused to be ensnared. Armed with the ability to make informed decisions rather than lingering in ignorance, she stood her ground, no longer a victim to his manipulations.

How Do You Transform from Victimhood to Survival?

Traumatic events possess the profound ability to reshape our connections with ourselves, others, and the world. Initially we may find ourselves overwhelmed by the agony, losing sight of our inner resilience. This state of vulnerability often necessitates nurturing and support, because we may feel negative emotions and endure profound suffering during this period. Persistent expression of this mindset can foster a sense of victimhood, where we perceive ourselves as powerless in the face of circumstances. Although this identification with victimhood may initially validate our pain, it is increasingly difficult to disentangle from this mindset over time. Consequently, what was once perceived as an external incident evolves into an integral aspect of our identity as we become defined by the role of victim.

However, lingering in this state impedes our sense of empowerment, as we resign ourselves to the suffering and forfeit the capacity to surmount it. This inertia thwarts any genuine progress, leaving us ensnared in anguish, yearning for a rescuer to alter our destiny. People often describe feeling stagnant, unable to move beyond a specific loss, event, or trauma. What perpetuates this feeling is an excessive identification with that particular circumstance, rather than recognizing it as merely one facet of their existence. By reclaiming a sense of agency, we can shed this stuck feeling and regain control over our life.

This emotional numbness is a protective mechanism employed by the mind to shield us from the overwhelming intensity of emotional pain. In this state, we may feel detached from our emotions, as if we are observing our experiences from a distance. This detachment serves as a temporary respite, allowing us to function despite the inner turmoil. However, while numbness may offer a brief reprieve, it can also inhibit the healing process by preventing us from fully acknowledging and processing our emotions. The goal of therapy or self-reflection is to gradually thaw this emotional freeze by gently exploring and validating the underlying feelings, allowing us to reintegrate our emotions and reclaim a sense of wholeness. This journey of healing requires patience, compassion, and often the support of a trusted therapist or counselor to provide empathy and validation along the way. Through this process, we can gradually reconnect with our emotions, regain trust in our ability to feel and withstand those emotions, and move forward on the path to healing and personal growth.

Regrettably, many people approach traumatic events without a clear strategy, hoping that time will simply mend their wounds. However, relying solely on time does not ensure healing and may even exacerbate the pain if it is not addressed effectively. Consequently, these people often find themselves engulfed in inner turmoil, yearning for something or someone to rescue them from their anguish. This hope becomes projected onto the first person who demonstrates desire and consistency in offering support, effectively becoming the rescuer. The issue arises when we remain ensnared in the victim role, unable to transition into the role of a survivor. By perpetuating this dynamic, we become dependent on the rescuer, relinquishing our own sense of agency. While seeking support from others is a natural inclination, finding solace in their presence should lead to mutual interdependence rather than continued dependency.

The enduring impact of a traumatic experience is perhaps most daunting in the powerlessness that persists long after the event. Unable to escape or evade the experience, we internalize a profound helplessness, feeling utterly devoid of control. Recovery from trauma entails the arduous task of reclaiming this lost power and reinstating faith in ourselves. Central to this process is surrender, a concept that is often misconstrued. In this context, it entails acknowledging the reality of the event without feeling it as an injustice. Surrender is an act of acceptance rather than resignation to the pain.

Understanding surrender in the context of navigating trauma requires a nuanced perspective that distinguishes between the traumatic event itself and the accompanying emotions. When we refer to surrender in this context, we're focusing on acknowledging the event rather than the psychological distress it generates. By recognizing that the event has taken place, we allow ourselves to experience the emotions related to it. This differentiation empowers us to acknowledge and manage our emotions effectively. If we blur the lines between the event and our identity, we may inadvertently adopt a victim mentality, perpetuating our suffering. However, by recognizing the event as separate from ourselves, we open the door to genuine healing and personal transformation.

Shifting your mindset is a process of understanding and altering ingrained thought patterns and beliefs. It begins with recognizing existing beliefs and thought habits, often through introspection and feedback from others. We can then challenge these beliefs by examining evidence, considering alternative perspectives, and actively reframing negative or limiting thoughts.

Practices such as cognitive restructuring and mindfulness play key roles in this process. Cognitive restructuring involves identifying and modifying unhelpful thought patterns, replacing them with more realistic and positive ones. Mindfulness techniques, such as meditation and self-awareness practices, help us observe our thoughts and emotions without judgment, fostering greater clarity and emotional regulation.

Consistency and practice are essential for lasting mindset shifts.

By consistently applying these techniques and incorporating new perspectives, we can gradually reshape our mindset toward a more positive, growth-oriented, and resilient outlook on life.

Reclaiming Your Strength and Shaping a New Narrative

Transitioning from a victim mindset to that of a survivor is a profound and empowering journey, one that requires deep introspection, deliberate action, and a commitment to personal growth. Below is a guide to help you navigate this transformative process in your own life.

The first step is recognizing the mindset that holds you in a place of disempowerment. Ask yourself which aspects of your thinking reflect a victim mentality? Consider your responses to adversity. Do you feel powerless or as though life is happening to you, rather than through you? If your instinctive response to setbacks is to think, *This always happens to me* or *There's nothing I can do*, this is a sign of victim thinking. Begin to challenge these reflexive thoughts by asking what you can learn from this situation and how you might regain control. By shifting your focus to potential growth, you begin to disrupt the victim mindset and open yourself to new possibilities.

Our beliefs shape our reality. Reflect on the internal narratives that you hold about yourself and your abilities. Are these beliefs limiting or empowering? The stories we tell ourselves often influence whether we view ourselves as victims or survivors. If you catch yourself thinking, *I'm not strong enough to overcome this*, begin the process of reframing by recalling moments of past resilience. Affirm instead, *I have faced hardship before and emerged stronger*. Writing down personal victories, no matter how small, can serve as a powerful reminder of your inherent strength and capability.

Ownership is the antidote to victimhood. Ask yourself what it would look like to fully take responsibility for your thoughts, feelings, and actions. True empowerment begins when you acknowledge that while you cannot control external circumstances, you can control your responses to them. If your initial reaction to adversity is *This isn't fair*, shift your perspective to *What can I do to move forward?* Ownership does not mean disregarding the validity of your pain, but it does mean refusing to let it define your future. Begin by making one small, intentional choice each day—whether it's setting a boundary, prioritizing your mental health, or taking proactive steps to address a challenge.

Identify the strengths and qualities you possess that can aid you in overcoming challenges. What are your inner resources that can be activated in moments of adversity? Perhaps your strength lies in your resilience, empathy, or problem-solving abilities. Reflect on a recent challenge where you demonstrated one of these strengths. If you've navigated through adversity before, trust that you can do so again. The key is to recognize that the very traits that helped you survive in the past are the same ones that will carry you forward.

Survivors understand that healing and empowerment are not solitary journeys. Who in your life provides the support and encouragement you need to move forward? Identifying your network of allies is crucial to maintaining momentum. Recognize the people in your life who uplift you—whether friends, family, mentors, or therapists. Make it a practice to reach out when you feel vulnerable. For instance, if you find yourself overwhelmed, call someone who has consistently offered you encouragement. Accepting help is not a sign of weakness, but rather an act of strength that reinforces your journey toward empowerment.

Victims dwell on what has been lost; survivors focus on what can be built. What goals or aspirations do you have that align with a mindset of growth? Rather than focusing on the setbacks you've faced, create a roadmap for how you can rise above them. For instance, if a personal or professional goal seems out of reach due to current circumstances, break it down into small, actionable steps. Celebrate progress, no matter how incremental, and acknowledge that each step forward is a testament to your resilience and determination.

Adversity often brings unexpected lessons. How can you cultivate a sense of gratitude for the challenges you've faced, recognizing the strengths they've helped you develop? Begin a gratitude practice that focuses specifically on lessons learned from difficult experiences. For instance, if a relationship ended painfully, reflect on how that hardship taught you to set healthier boundaries. By acknowledging the growth that arises from struggle, you reframe adversity as a catalyst for transformation rather than an obstacle.

The ability to remain present and mindful is critical in shifting from a reactive state to a proactive one. What steps can you take to stay grounded and centered when faced with challenges? Incorporate mindfulness techniques, such as breathwork or meditation, into your daily routine. When anxiety or negative thoughts arise, focus on grounding yourself in the present moment. For example, practice deep breathing when you feel overwhelmed, reminding yourself, *This moment is temporary, and I have the tools to navigate it.*

Shifting from victim to survivor requires consistent reinforcement of empowering narratives. What affirmations or mantras can you use to support your growth? Create affirmations that reflect your evolving strength. Repeat phrases such as "I am resilient and capable of overcoming any challenge," or "Each day, I choose growth and empowerment." Practice saying these affirmations aloud, especially when you face moments of doubt. Over time, these positive reinforcements will help reshape your inner dialogue and solidify your survivor mindset.

16

Good Versus Evil

Charlotte had been back home for days, but there was an unsettling silence from Adam. He had sent flowers to her office with a generic note welcoming her back, but there had been no direct communication from him. She found herself constantly staring at her phone, hoping for any form of contact—only to be disappointed. It was difficult to comprehend how he could stay away after the magical time they had shared in London. She wondered what could have triggered such a cold response—or the lack of a response at all. She analyzed every moment they had spent together, overthinking every word, glance, and gesture, trying to pinpoint whether she had done or said something to drive him away. This was one of the aspects she despised about having Adam in her life—the lack of clarity. He always left her questioning their connection and, worst of all, herself.

Feeling overwhelmed, she settled on the loveseat at the foot of her bed. The room was shrouded in darkness, the fading sunset casting a reddish hue in the corner. She had no desire to turn on the lights; all she craved was solitude, an opportunity to confront the demons within her and understand why she'd willingly subjected herself to this misery once again. She gazed at herself in the mirror, feeling old. She searched her face for the cause of this change. Her eyes. They were cold and vacant, devoid of life.

Her mind traveled back to the aftermath of her car accident. As she woke from surgery, the haze of anesthesia clouded her thoughts. She found herself in a hospital bed, in pain and confusion. Tentatively, she touched her face and felt the bandage there. She tried to sit up, her body aching. The physical pain faded into insignificance as she remembered her profound loss. This pain cut deeper. For a moment, she empathized with her patients who turned to self-harm as a means to endure emotional agony. It made perfect sense to her. Physical pain was manageable, with a clear source and potential treatment; but the darkness that consumed her soul was overwhelming. How could she even begin to understand it herself, let alone explain it to others? And how could such an intangible pain ever be healed?

Charlotte felt disbelief, akin to what Elizabeth Kübler-Ross referred to as denial.[8] She kept searching her mind for the possibility of it being a bad dream, imagining it hadn't really happened. She had watched a show in her mind, saw a character

---

8 Elizabeth Kübler-Ross, *On Death and Dying* (Macmillan, 1969).

return alive after months of agony for the survivors. She wondered, *What if my father is alive too? If he is truly gone, I need to see the body*. Her mind clung to hope; the reality was too much. She struggled with the emptiness, and the certainty of never having closure gnawed at her.

She summoned the nurse and requested a mirror. She recalled the doctor showing her the extent of the damage to her face before the surgery, explaining that he would do his best to salvage as much of her facial features as possible. The thought of resembling a monster sent a shiver down her spine, but even that paled in comparison to the pain of her loss. There were no familiar faces in the room, and she assumed her family was preoccupied elsewhere. Although she felt lonely, she was relieved that no one was there to see her changed features before she had a chance to see herself.

With the mirror in her hands, she gathered the courage to confront her reflection. Taking a deep breath, she slowly turned the mirror around and faced herself. Her face was marred with heavy bruising, cuts, and scrapes from the shattered glass. The left side of her face was completely bandaged, and her long hair had been shaved, leaving a distinct demarcation just beyond her forehead. It was undoubtedly an unpleasant sight, but what pierced her heart the most was the pain in her eyes—or, rather, her right eye. The left eye remained hidden beneath the bandages, but her right eye appeared aged, as if it had weathered a decade's turmoil overnight. A dull and vacant expression had replaced the vibrant curiosity she had once seen there. She realized that she had come face-to-face with the cruelty, darkness, and malevolence of the real world.

Once that dark side of life is faced, it can never be forgotten. The evil of negativity lurks within every moment and every individual. Just as with any other opposing forces in life, it coexists with the positive—what we commonly refer to as goodness. These contrasting aspects are the dual sides of life.

In that moment, Charlotte confronted the depths of the evil side. With its merciless power, it tore her family asunder, leaving her profoundly devastated. The frigid look in her eyes confirmed that this negative force, once it is activated, transcends external circumstances. It seeps into the depths of your soul, becoming intertwined with your internalized sense of self. In its grip, the ability to perceive your surroundings with unwavering positivity is lost. You can take on a state of perpetual anticipation for the next attack. Life becomes infused with fear, and that fear dominates every moment. Your energy shifts, tilting the balance more toward pain than harmony. Strangely, this distressing choice becomes increasingly seductive, ensnaring you in a repetitive cycle without escape.

Back in the present moment, Charlotte gently traced her healed scar with her fingertips, observing it in the mirror. Years had passed, and the physical wounds had faded to the point that they were almost imperceptible to others. The pain of the accident and the subsequent events had become a distant memory. She had adapted to the loss, and her family had found ways to move forward. However, one aspect remained unchanged: the emotional turmoil. The accident had awakened a fearful presence within her, stripping away her sense of choice and trapping her in a constant anticipation of disaster.

Sitting in the darkness, Charlotte wondered whether her connection with Adam would have taken root if her life had unfolded differently. It was challenging to discern whether her attraction to him was a consequence of fear or a conscious decision. Did her feelings for him stem from love, or were they merely a response to her wounded state? Did she subject herself to this pain because she genuinely loved him, or did the broken part within her choose him as a means of self-punishment for surviving? She inclined toward the latter, considering the immense pain their relationship had caused her. Deep within, her higher self recognized that love should not inflict harm. Love should be kind, compassionate, and nurturing. But when a person gravitates toward another from a place of hurt, it perpetuates further pain.

Charlotte had first encountered Adam not long after her accident, sensing a soothing power in him that pacified her fearful vulnerability. She acknowledged that her trauma had triggered an unhealthy mechanism of self-punishment. She understood that if she didn't take charge of the situation and actively seek healing, she would exhaust her chances of growth and remain in this unsettling state. As she finally rose to prepare for bed, the clock striking 3 a.m., she was exhausted. The next day held a demanding schedule, leaving no room for further sleep deprivation. Closing her eyes, she visualized herself strong enough to resist the allure of dysfunction. Forgetting Adam was not her goal; she wanted to outgrow him by reconnecting with her true self and loving herself enough to release anything that no longer served her.

Charlotte understood the complexity of healing all too well, both as someone enduring the process and as a therapist trained to guide others through it. Every time she thought she had moved beyond Adam, she found herself pulled back into the same cycle, as if the emotional scar tissue never fully healed but instead lay dormant, waiting to resurface. Layer by layer, she peeled back the remnants of her past trauma, only to encounter another. It frustrated her deeply, this recurring realization that she hadn't yet broken free. But in the quiet hours of reflection, her professional self would remind her that healing is not a singular, linear event.

Scientifically, Charlotte knew that the brain's response to trauma operates within a framework of neural pathways that become reinforced over time, particularly when emotions like fear, guilt, and shame are involved. The amygdala, the brain's center for emotional processing, often triggers the fight-or-flight response long after the initial event has passed. And though she had consciously worked on releasing Adam, the deeply ingrained neural patterns associated with her attachment to him continued to fire. Each time she believed she had conquered this emotional tie, she encountered a resurgence, not because she was weak, but because those pathways hadn't yet fully dissolved.

Charlotte also recognized that neuroplasticity, the brain's ability to rewire itself, required repetition. She reminded herself that every encounter with Adam, whether literal or in her mind, was an opportunity to reshape her internal landscape. Yet, the process brought up shame and guilt—feelings that were hard to shake. How could she, someone who had facilitated countless patients' healing, continue to struggle with the same recurring attachment? She had to acknowledge the guilt that arose from the cognitive dissonance between her therapist identity and her lived experience, and the shame of not having fully transcended these patterns.

However, she understood that this was the nature of complex trauma; it wasn't something one could "beat" in a single epiphany or through mere willpower. Trauma often reemerged, sometimes unexpectedly, when triggered by familiar emotions, smells, or even fleeting thoughts. The hippocampus, where emotional memories are stored, isn't as easily persuaded to let go.

With this knowledge, Charlotte knew that each step in her journey, even the regressions, served a purpose. Healing was iterative. It was a process of reengaging with the same wound, but from a slightly different vantage point each time, strengthening new neural pathways and weakening old ones. She had to remind herself, with compassion, that true healing involved returning to the same point of pain repeatedly, not out of failure, but because that was how growth happened—incrementally, slowly.

What kept her grounded in this process was the understanding that her work was not to forget Adam or rid herself of her past but to outgrow them. Integration, not elimination, was the key. To reclaim her narrative meant to love herself enough to understand that these layers of hurt weren't simply setbacks;

they were stepping stones. She wasn't going backward—she was circling deeper into the core of herself, where the roots of her trauma lay.

Charlotte knew that each reemergence of the past was a new opportunity to tackle it with more insight and compassion than the last. This wasn't the shame of defeat; it was the complexity of healing in motion. Her professional self knew this intimately, but her vulnerable self was still learning to accept it. And as exhausting as the process was, Charlotte held on to the fact that it was this very process that would one day set her free.

In this light, she viewed her relationship with Adam not as a failure to overcome, but as a mirror, reflecting the unresolved parts of her inner world. She wasn't just trying to let him go; she was unraveling the very neural and emotional pathways that had bound her to him, and that took time. This was the cyclical nature of self-discovery: clarity, regression, repeat, until one day, the cycle no longer had power over her.

Exhausted by these thoughts, Charlotte decided to lie down, hoping that sleep might bring her some reprieve. When she awoke, Charlotte discovered a text from Tarek, who had also returned, welcoming her home and inviting her to dinner. Just as she began considering the possibility of moving forward, her fingers instinctively typing her response, a message from Adam appeared, confessing dreams of her and expressing his longing. Her heart sank, but this time the impact was different. The glare of emotional entanglement had dulled. She dismissed the idea of accepting Tarek's invitation. How could she move on when she was still confused? She saw through Adam's games and recognized the incongruity with her own needs. Despite the desire to respond to Adam, she acknowledged the truth behind his message and refrained from replying, setting her phone aside before stepping into the shower.

As the water cascaded over her, Charlotte smiled at the notion of exerting power over her own choices, opting to walk away from what she deemed undesirable. Empowerment surged within her, and she knew that, despite the magnetic pull she felt toward Adam, she could break free and embrace a different path. Despite having only slept four hours, she was filled with vibrant energy. Dressing for work, she caught a glimpse of herself in the mirror and discovered a playful twinkle in her eyes that hadn't been there the night before.

Reconciling the Struggle Between Light and Shadow

In most religious, philosophical, and psychological literature, the concept of good and evil is often used to depict the dualistic nature of human beings and the conflicts that arise within themselves and in relation to others. As humans navigate through life's ups and downs, they exhibit a spectrum of behaviors. In an attempt to understand these actions, we tend to oversimplify them by labeling them as good or evil. In essence, we label what benefits us as good and what harms us as bad. However, this categorization leads to a dangerous game of labeling individuals as inherently good or evil based solely on their behavior.

Given the complexity of human nature, it is fair to say that behavior cannot be neatly categorized into such binary domains. We must allow for the fluidity and nuance within what is labeled as good or evil. Empathy seems to be the yardstick by which this dynamic is measured among humans. The more someone is capable of prioritizing the needs and desires of others above their own and chooses to behave selflessly, the more society labels them as good. Conversely, when a person displays egocentric behavior devoid of empathy, they are labeled as evil. The truth is that all of us have the potential to exhibit both types of behavior, depending on our circumstances and capacities at any given time.

The problem with this duality lies in its subjective nature. When we label something, we are viewing it from our own perspective. In reality, what may be considered good for us could be perceived as evil by someone else. This polarity makes it nearly impossible to have a universal notion of benevolence. What may benefit one group could be detrimental to others. As such, good and evil are not always appropriate classifications, and most of life exists as a blend of various shades.

So why do we constantly feel the need to judge and label our own behavior and that of others in such dichotomous terms? If we reflect on it, much of our perceived pain stems from these judgments and evaluations. We are all seeking to protect ourselves from perceived harm, so we continuously assess people and circumstances to ensure our safety. As soon as we sense any potential danger to our physical or emotional well-being, our fear response is triggered, putting us in fight-or-flight mode. However, these reactions are often extreme responses based on our cumulative life experiences and the inherited patterns passed down through generations.

This notion of an easy dichotomy extends beyond the realm of individual behavior to encompass the nuanced dynamics of life circumstances. As we navigate various situations, events, and experiences, our tendency to categorize them as inherently good or evil is a simplification that often overlooks their complexities. Rarely do life's events unfold in a binary fashion; even ostensibly positive experiences can carry hidden challenges, while seemingly adverse circumstances may contain latent opportunities or invaluable insights. This recognition underscores the multifaceted nature of human existence, urging us to embrace a more nuanced perspective that acknowledges the interplay of light and shadow, success and adversity, within the fabric of our lives.

The yin and yang symbol, rooted in Taoist philosophy, serves as a profound metaphor for the complexities of life's circumstances. Its divided circle, with black (yin) and white (yang) halves intertwined and complemented by small dots of the opposite color, encapsulates the essence of duality and interconnectedness. In our experiences, this symbol resonates deeply, reminding us that life's events are rarely purely good or bad, but rather a delicate balance of contrasting forces.

Just as yin and yang harmonize to create a whole, our positive experiences often contain hidden challenges, while adversities may harbor unexpected opportunities for growth and learning. The dynamic nature of the symbol's swirling motion reflects the ever-evolving nature of our circumstances, urging us to embrace life's complexity and appreciate the interplay of light and shadow that shapes our journey.

In our pursuit of self-preservation, we habitually judge, evaluate, and maneuver to protect ourselves and ensure survival. While some of our assessments are justified and prevent us from engaging in undesired situations, many of our responses are rooted in trauma and stem from less evolved emotional processes. The more mature systems within us can remain neutral and nonreactive. The truth is that people around us rarely fall into the extreme ends of the spectrum of good and evil. What we perceive in them is often a projection of our inner reactions to their behavior. Most of us fall somewhere in the middle, exhibiting a range of behaviors that fluctuate based on mood and circumstances but that rarely reach the extremes that experts would label as clinically significant.

Our tendency to categorize people who benefit us as good and those who hurt us as bad causes us to become victims of certain beliefs and surrender our own role and power within the dynamic. It would benefit us to view others and ourselves in a more realistic light, recognizing that we are capable of displaying a mixture of various responses at any given time. After all, it is this versatility that defines the human experience.

Balancing Your Dual Nature Through Self-Understanding

Nonbinary categorization refers to the practice of moving away from rigid, either/or thinking in how we view ourselves, others, and experiences. Often, we are conditioned to place things in simple categories—good or bad, right or wrong, success or failure. However, life is far more complex, and by learning to approach people, situations, and decisions with greater nuance, we can cultivate deeper understanding, empathy, and flexibility. Below, you will learn how to challenge binary thinking and embrace a nonbinary perspective in various aspects of life.

One common way we engage in binary thinking is by categorizing ourselves as either strong or weak in certain areas. This can limit our self-perception, causing us to label aspects of ourselves as either purely positive or negative. To move beyond this, start recognizing the complexity in your abilities and areas for growth. Instead of viewing yourself as "bad" at public speaking because you're uncomfortable in front of crowds, acknowledge that you have the potential to grow in this area with practice. Rather than labeling yourself as "weak" in communication, you can say, *I'm improving my communication skills*. This small shift helps you see growth as a continuous process, not a fixed trait.

Binary thinking can also shape how we view others, often leading to judgments based on first impressions or limited information. Instead of categorizing people as "friendly" or "unfriendly," "good" or "bad," challenge yourself to see the multifaceted nature of each person you encounter. Next time you meet someone, try to avoid making snap judgments based on a single interaction. Instead, stay open and curious. Someone who may seem aloof in one moment might be shy or reserved, and that doesn't define them entirely. By approaching others with empathy and curiosity, you allow for deeper connections and a better understanding of their complexities.

A nonbinary approach encourages us to stop viewing experiences strictly as successes or failures. Every situation offers the potential for learning, growth, and adaptation. Reframing this allows you to focus on the lessons gained from an experience rather than labeling it as simply "good" or "bad." If you didn't get the job you applied for, instead of viewing this as a failure, reflect on what you learned from the process. Did it improve your interview skills? Did you gain clarity about the kind of job you want? By framing setbacks as opportunities for growth, you avoid the trap of binary thinking and instead focus on how each experience contributes to your overall journey.

In moments of conflict, binary thinking often takes the form of viewing things as right versus wrong or good versus bad. This mindset can create unnecessary tension and hinder resolution. Instead, consider approaching conflicts with a more nuanced perspective, recognizing that different viewpoints and intentions coexist. When facing a disagreement, instead of trying to "win" an argument, take a step back and consider the other person's perspective. Ask yourself, *What factors are influencing their opinion?* By acknowledging the complexity of the situation and seeking to understand all sides, you open the door to empathy and constructive dialogue.

Binary thinking can make decision-making feel like a choice between two rigid options: this or that. However, most decisions can be approached with a spectrum of possibilities and alternatives. By embracing the complexity of decision-making, you open yourself up to more creative and effective outcomes. When faced with a decision—such as whether to take on a new project or not—explore the middle ground. Can you negotiate your workload to take on part of the project, or can it be done in phases? By thinking beyond simple yes or no choices, you create space for compromise and innovative solutions.

Our language plays a powerful role in reinforcing binary thinking. Words like *always*, *never*, *good*, *bad*, *right*, and *wrong* can limit our ability to engage with the complexity of situations. Adjusting your language to reflect nuanced thinking is essential for fostering more inclusive, open-minded communication. Instead of saying, "You always do this" in a relationship conflict, which frames the situation in absolutes, try "I've noticed this happens sometimes, and I want to talk about it." This shift in language makes room for dialogue and avoids placing the other person into an oversimplified category, leading to more productive conversations.

From Binary to Open-Minded

When our beliefs or assumptions are challenged, we may feel compelled to defend them rigidly. This can trap us in binary thinking, where we see our perspective as "right" and others as "wrong." Embracing ambiguity means being willing to accept that multiple truths can coexist and that we don't always have to be certain. If a new piece of information contradicts a long-held belief, instead of rejecting it outright, try considering it with an open mind. For example, if someone offers a perspective on an issue that differs from yours, reflect on how their lived experience shapes their view. You don't have to abandon your beliefs, but you can learn to hold them more lightly and be open to the idea that they might evolve over time.

To expand your ability to think non-binarily, actively seek out diverse perspectives and experiences that challenge your biases and assumptions. Exposure to different viewpoints helps you recognize the complexity of issues and people, and reduces the tendency to think in black-and-white terms. Engage with media, books, and conversations that offer perspectives different from your own. If you are accustomed to reading a particular genre or viewpoint, explore something outside your usual scope. By exposing yourself to a wider range of ideas, you train your mind to embrace complexity and reject simplistic categorization.

Whether in personal relationships or work settings, fostering open dialogue, empathy, and understanding across different viewpoints is essential to moving beyond binary thinking. Create spaces where people feel safe to express their full, multidimensional selves without fear of being boxed into rigid categories. In group discussions, encourage others to share their diverse viewpoints and create an atmosphere of respect. When someone expresses a different perspective, respond with openness rather than judgment. This builds an inclusive environment where multiple ideas can coexist and be explored without pressure to conform to a binary way of thinking.

Finally, cultivating mindfulness allows you to be present with your thoughts and emotions without rushing to categorize them. By practicing non-judgmental awareness, you can approach life's complexities with curiosity and acceptance, appreciating the diversity and richness of human experience. When a strong emotion arises, instead of labeling it as "good" or "bad," observe it without judgment. Ask yourself, *What can I learn from this feeling?* This practice allows you to engage with your emotions in a deeper, more meaningful way, without the need to classify them as purely positive or negative.

17

Revenge Versus Forgiveness

Charlotte had spent the entire day shuttling between doctor's appointments. She usually tried to alleviate the monotony of these visits by maintaining excellent self-care and a healthy lifestyle. However, despite her diligent efforts, she could no longer overlook the intense pain in her left ribcage. As she sat with the fourth doctor of the day, she felt her heartbeat intensify. Until this moment, she hadn't seriously considered the possibility of a health issue. Now, facing the probing of the doctor, she began to feel a rising anxiety.

The doctor kept his gaze on her labs and murmured, "Have you ever had an injury to this part of your body?"

Charlotte was about to respond with her routine "no" when she quickly recalled the accident. So she slowly said, "Ten years ago, I was in a car accident. The left side of my body was hit badly at impact." She felt her mouth get dry as she said that, so she tried swallowing to trigger a salivating response.

The doctor looked up and said, "I can't say for sure until we open it up, but it seems like built-up scar tissue from an old injury."

Charlotte felt a shiver in her left hand as he began to speak, which she covered with her right hand and nervously asked, "Is surgery necessary?" The idea of ending up back in the hospital after everything that had happened truly frightened her.

The doctor coldly shrugged his shoulder as he closed her chart and mumbled, "If you want to get rid of the pain, then yes."

Charlotte walked out of the office in dismay. She took her phone out of her bag to call a friend when she saw an incoming call from Adam. In this moment of weakness, she responded. They exchanged pleasantries, and he asked why she hadn't called him. She casually alluded to her health issues, and his voice became very serious. He asked where she was and if they could meet up. Charlotte reluctantly agreed; maybe it was her fear of what was happening or the need to be around a familiar presence, but despite her hesitation, something inside her craved the comfort Adam once offered. She knew it wasn't the best choice—she had almost called a friend, someone who could give her the support she needed without the emotional baggage. But Adam, with all the complications he brought, was a familiar presence, and right now, familiarity felt like safety. There was a powerful pull toward him, a draw that felt almost addictive, as if she couldn't fully escape the old patterns they'd built together.

It wasn't just comfort she sought; it was the particular comfort Adam had once provided, even though she knew deep down it wasn't good for her anymore. The reluctance lingered, but the longing for that fleeting sense of solace won out, leaving her torn between logic and the emotional need to feel safe, even if it meant turning back to someone she had tried so hard to move on from. Also, it was unlike Adam to drop everything like that and just show up, which made her even more impressed.

They met at a local bar. As he walked in, he rushed to her and held her close. His grip around her tightened as he asked her about her health. She explained the situation, and with every word, his face grew more and more concerned. He took his phone out and began to dial a number, ordering his secretary to get an appointment from a doctor. Then he told Charlotte that he knew a very good surgeon and that he would take her to see him for a second opinion.

Charlotte felt his warm touch on her hand and looked down; he was gripping both her hands with his. His touch was so solid and so warm that, for a second, Charlotte forgot all about his inconsistency. She closed her eyes, feeling the loneliness of having to go through this by herself slip away. She had so many unmet wishes; in moments of weakness, her vulnerability would surface and give away her true needs. She wished her life had unfolded differently; she wished Adam would be more transparent. More than anything, she wished she had the power to just walk away and not need him in this moment.

Tears started to roll down her face. Adam reached out and wiped them away and held her head to his chest, giving her tiny kisses on the top of her head and stroking her hair with his fingers. She stayed there for a bit as her sobs intensified. He comforted her, and at one point, she could feel him starting to shake a bit. She pulled herself back and looked up; his eyes were also wet. She looked at him with a puzzled gaze.

He smiled and said, "I'm sorry." It was as if he had read her mind, apologizing for what he couldn't be. It was almost as though he knew exactly how much he had hurt her but had demons of his own, making him unable to completely disengage from her yet just as reluctant to properly commit to a relationship.

They both took a moment to regain their composure, suddenly very aware that they were in a public place. They exchanged a glance pregnant with a thousand words, but they said little for the remainder of the evening. It was one of those nights in which silence explained more than words.

The next few days were filled with emotion. Earlier in the week, Adam had arranged for a second opinion from a specialist, hoping to explore every possible option. However, after speaking with multiple doctors, including Adam's chosen specialist, it was confirmed that the original recommendation was indeed the best course of action.

Charlotte made the arrangements for her upcoming surgery, and Adam stayed by her side the entire time. It seemed like he had gone back to being the kind, loving soul she knew. The day before her surgery, Charlotte was finishing up some last-minute details in her home office, and Adam had stopped by to see her. Charlotte had to respond to an emergency call, and Adam offered to make some tea and meet her on the balcony a bit later.

Charlotte finished her call sooner than expected and walked

out to the balcony. Adam was sitting on a chair with his back to her, talking on the phone. He could not see her. As she stepped outside, she heard him say, "I love you too. See you soon."

Charlotte felt her heart drop in her chest. Her feet were glued to the ground. She stood there for what felt like an eternity and tried to process her next move. Her mouth felt dry; she tried to hold back a cough, but she couldn't. At the sound, Adam turned to her, his gaze filled with surprise.

Their eyes locked for a while. They both knew this was the moment of truth. She knew she had to say something, so she simply said, "I cannot begin to deal with this again, especially at this point in my life. I need you to leave and never come back."

She pointed to the door and looked away from him. Her voice was so firm and explicit, she surprised herself.

He tried to approach her, but she stepped back. He stood there for a bit and slowly began walking toward the door, and she followed. As he placed his hand on the doorknob, he looked back and said, "Let my driver take you to your surgery tomorrow."

Charlotte murmured, "No thank you."

As he closed the door behind him, Charlotte walked back out to the balcony. She could see him exit the building and get into his car and leave. She tried to memorize every movement because she knew this would be the last time she would ever see him. Part of her wanted to keep loving him, another part of her wanted to hate him for deceiving her, and the rest of her felt sadness and shame for letting him treat her as he did. A whirlpool of emotions dragged her from one side to the other.

Some moments mark the end of an era, altering the course of life irreversibly. She had encountered a few such transformative junctures, vivid among them those final moments in the car before the accident, where her parents' words about their dreams and aspirations seemed to hang in the air, only to be shattered in an instant. In hindsight, she wished for a whisper of warning, a chance to brace herself for the impending storm. But she found herself facing another pivotal moment, where she drew a line in the sand, setting a boundary: She was done with Adam. Although it was tinged with melancholy, this act of assertion brought with it a liberation—a nuanced blend of sorrow and newfound resolve.

After their previous breakup, she had remained frozen in pain for months, still worshiping him. The loss had paralyzed her. Then she had gone through a phase of hating him for what he had done, keeping herself in a state of agony for trusting him. The emotional torment had lasted for months, and she felt miserable every minute of every day.

This time around, she knew better. He was simply a human being—with all the virtues and flaws of the rest of us. He was someone she'd shared a segment of her life with, hoping for a happily-ever-after yet realizing that was not in the stars. She felt a pain run through her body, the kind of disappointment you feel after you realize a dream you had hoped for is not going to come true.

The sensation felt achingly familiar, stirring deeply buried memories. Charlette closed her eyes, transported back to a day tinged with sorrow, the day after her release from the hospital. Despite her frailty, an undeniable restlessness gnawed at her soul, urging her to seek solace in her father's presence.

She pleaded and bargained with those arranging the funeral, desperate to be taken to him. They tried to refuse her, but she stormed into the morgue, demanding to see him. Beneath the white shroud lay her father, still and silent. Her trembling hand lingered on the fabric, yearning for a miracle that would erase the reality before her.

This was not the final moment—his body had yet to be prepared for burial. It was still the morgue, the threshold before the purification, where he remained untouched by the ritual hands that would cleanse him and ready him for his final passage. This space, suspended between life and death, was a liminal realm, a stark confrontation with reality. It was a biopsy of her grief, a dissection of disbelief and reluctant acceptance, peeling back the layers of hope she had yet to surrender.

As she lifted the sheet, his familiar face greeted her, a bittersweet reunion marred by bruises and cuts. His left side was ravaged and broken, mirroring her own injuries. His impact had been fatal, hers a cruel survivor's tale. She gently traced his features, unable to bid farewell. "Until we meet again," she murmured, covering him with the sheet once more.

There on the balcony, as she watched Adam's car disappear from view, Charlotte found herself whispering those same words to the wind, a silent vow echoing through the emptiness left by loss. Her lips quivered with a silent cry, but there was no destruction or suffering with the sadness. She thought about it but was not consumed by it. Her inner critic was also kinder than usual. She had tried, given him one more chance. He failed, and she accepted the loss—no more harsh self-talk of *What were you thinking trusting him again? It serves you right!*

She simply felt compassion and understanding for her needs and desires. She stood there until the sun started to set, thinking about how far she had come in processing her emotions, proud of her ability to take chances and move on gracefully when they proved to be a wrong choice.

What struck her most profoundly was her absence of animosity toward him. Despite the pain he had inflicted, she harbored no resentment. It brought to mind the anger her family had expressed toward the other driver, calling for retribution. While she could relate to that sentiment to a certain extent, she held no ill will toward the other driver, as if she intuitively recognized him as someone who had simply made a horrible mistake. And now, she felt no vitriol for Adam. Instead, she chose to embody the profound wisdom that forgiveness is not about condoning the actions of others but about freeing yourself from the chains of anger and resentment.

Is Seeking Revenge Worth the Emotional Cost?

From a psychological perspective, revenge and forgiveness represent contrasting responses to perceived wrongdoings or injustices, each carrying its own emotional, cognitive, and behavioral weight. Revenge is often fueled by intense emotions like anger, resentment, and the thirst for retribution. These emotions can consume us, leading to rumination and vengeful thoughts that contribute to increased stress and negative mood states. The cognitive processes involved in seeking revenge can be characterized by a fixation on the offense and a desire to restore justice or regain control, often resulting in behaviors ranging from verbal aggression to more extreme acts of retaliation. However, while revenge may offer temporary satisfaction, it can also perpetuate cycles of conflict and hinder personal growth in the long run.

On the other hand, forgiveness involves a profound emotional shift from anger and bitterness to empathy, compassion, and understanding. It requires us to let go of negative emotions, reframe our cognitive perspective, and focus on positive aspects such as empathy, reconciliation, and personal growth. Forgiveness is associated with prosocial behaviors, improved mental health, reduced stress, and enhanced relationship satisfaction. Choosing forgiveness can promote psychological well-being, foster healthier relationships, and contribute to personal growth and resilience.

When it comes to revenge and forgiveness, the crucial factor that shapes our path is the concept of blame. When we undergo tormenting pain, we often seek to assign blame to someone else. This blame game sets off a chain reaction of agonizing psychological turmoil, leaving us fragile and vulnerable to dehumanizing experiences. In such vulnerable states, we often fixate on pinpointing the origin of our pain, hoping to find solace. When we attribute this pain to another person, it can drive us to take drastic punitive actions, fueled by a misguided belief that it will ease our suffering. At other times, we become fixated and immobilized by the wrongs inflicted upon us by others. If this fixation persists, it can lead to prolonged traumatic experiences, compromising our ability to function effectively, potentially causing long-term damage. A critical step in overcoming psychological turmoil is restoring and strengthening the sense of self, aiming to return it to an optimal level of functionality, which often involves reclaiming lost empowerment.

When someone experiences emotional pain as a result of another person's wrongdoing, they tend to believe that the person causing the pain has gained power over them, indicating a loss of power on the victim's end. This state feels debilitating, so to recover from it, we have to regain our assertiveness. Revenge, although not always constructive, is an attempt to reclaim lost power. The key here is that most people focus on the other to recover from this pain, whereas true healing comes from rebuilding the self that feels destroyed.

While revenge can temporarily serve as a soothing mechanism, it does not heal the underlying wounds that trigger the pain. In fact, it has the tendency to leave us feeling even more empty and fragile. However, it can at times act as a motivating catalyst that brings movement to the recovery process. Nevertheless, what is truly effective is not doing something to another person but regaining our sense of power over them.

Displaying the consequences of someone's actions to them may be somewhat freeing, allowing the victim to feel enough ease to hopefully move on. The problem is this mindset is oriented outward, toward the other. Forgiveness is a self-oriented process that targets the ability to stop blaming, accept responsibility for what to do next, and let go of whatever no longer serves us. This is truly regaining power: accepting that no matter what a person does to you, they cannot influence what you choose to do next.

People simply give us information via their actions, and it is completely up to us to decide what we want to do with that knowledge. At times, what we learn makes us invest even more deeply in that person, and at other times, it makes us create space and detach. What matters is that we are the deciding agents of our own lives, and we have power over our own actions no matter what life throws at us. This position of power comes with a strong sense of self.

Take Responsibility and Feel Empowered

People often misconstrue taking responsibility as admitting fault. This misunderstanding implies that if I take responsibility for a situation, it means I am to blame for the wrongdoing against me by another person. However, this is not accurate. Taking responsibility does not absolve the wrongdoer of their responsibility but, rather, empowers the victim to regain control over their circumstances. The key is to sidestep the notion of blame altogether and to focus on empowering the victim to navigate their situation with agency and resilience.

If we can manage to remain in this psychological state during an emotionally dissatisfying situation, other people's actions, although painful at times, simply become an experience we work through and move on from when necessary. On the contrary, when we identify with the pain and lose our sense of self to it, we relinquish our power and become enslaved to the distress, which, in turn, makes us feel weaker and weaker until we completely feel powerless, not only with the situation at hand but also in our daily life.

There is a magical question that can shift our attention from freezing to taking action in times of psychological anguish. Ask yourself: *Given this circumstance, what can I do next?* This question takes the mind's focus from whatever the source of pain is back to the action-oriented self, reminding us of two important facts: First, that there is a next step or next stage, and our story does not end with this pain. Second, and more importantly, we have complete control over what happens next.

This mindset helps us take charge of a problem by moving into a space of action rather than remaining stuck in a cycle of blame. The essence of forgiveness lies in the ability to move forward. When we can successfully detach from a painful notion, it loses its grip on us, and the first step to moving on is planning the next step, rather than dwelling on the past.

Finding Peace Through Forgiveness

Shifting from a mindset rooted in revenge to one that embraces forgiveness is a transformative process that requires deep introspection, emotional resilience, and a commitment to personal growth. Seeking revenge often feels justified in moments of anger, but it comes at a cost. When you focus your energy on retaliation, it consumes your thoughts, keeps you locked in negative emotions, and drains your emotional resources. Someone who was betrayed by a trusted colleague becomes consumed with thoughts of getting even. Over time, they realize that constantly revisiting the betrayal and plotting revenge is affecting their sleep, mood, and ability to focus on other aspects of their life. By acknowledging the toll it takes on their well-being, they can begin to see the futility of revenge and shift their attention toward self-care.

Forgiveness is a tool for reclaiming your peace of mind, not a way of excusing harmful behavior. Letting go of resentment is an act of self-liberation that frees you from the emotional grip of the past. After a long-standing dispute, someone realizes that holding on to resentment is keeping them from enjoying life fully. Instead of continuously revisiting the pain, they make the decision to forgive—not to forget what happened but to regain control over their emotions and restore a sense of calm and balance.

Forgiveness can be a source of empowerment, allowing you to regain control over your emotional landscape. It shifts the power away from those who hurt you and places it back in your hands. Someone who has been hurt by a close friend initially feels powerless and seeks ways to retaliate. Upon reflection, they realize that forgiveness gives them the strength to move forward, without being trapped in the emotional spiral of blame. By reframing forgiveness as an act of personal power, they regain their sense of agency and emotional control.

Understanding the humanity of those who have hurt you can open the door to forgiveness. While it doesn't condone their actions, it allows you to see that their behavior often stems from their own struggles. After experiencing conflict with a family member, someone begins to recognize that the person's actions were not about them but were rooted in the family member's own unresolved pain and insecurities. By seeing the situation from this perspective, they feel more compassion and are able to approach forgiveness with a greater sense of understanding.

Forgiveness doesn't happen overnight, and it's important to be kind to yourself throughout the process. Acknowledging your pain and giving yourself time to heal is essential. Someone who was hurt in a romantic relationship feels pressure to "move on" quickly, but instead of rushing the process, they instead allow themselves the space to grieve and process their emotions. By practicing self-compassion, they begin to heal on their own terms, eventually reaching a place where forgiveness feels possible and authentic.

Acceptance is a crucial step in forgiveness. It doesn't mean condoning what happened, but it means acknowledging that the past can't be changed. This acceptance allows you to release the emotional burden. After a major life disappointment, someone may find themselves repeatedly going over what could have been done differently. Over time, they come to accept that the situation is beyond their control. This acceptance helps them focus on what they can change—how they choose to respond going forward—and allows them to let go of the bitterness attached to the event.

Once the desire for revenge is let go, that energy can be redirected into positive endeavors like personal growth, healing, or building new, meaningful connections. After a professional setback, someone initially feels the urge to retaliate against the person they blame for the outcome. Instead of acting on these impulses, they decide to invest their energy into improving their skills and pursuing new opportunities. This shift not only helps them grow but also leads to greater satisfaction and success than they would have achieved through revenge.

Adversity often provides valuable lessons. By reflecting on difficult experiences, you can learn more about yourself and build resilience for future challenges. After going through a challenging personal experience, you might reflect on how it helped you develop patience, emotional strength, and a greater sense of empathy for others. Instead of focusing on the negative aspects of the experience, you can see it as an opportunity for growth and self-discovery, which contributes to your long-term resilience.

Forgiveness is often made easier when you surround yourself with people who support your healing journey. A positive support network helps you stay focused on growth rather than resentment. Someone who has experienced betrayal seeks support from friends or mentors who encourage them to focus on their own well-being. These supportive individuals help others navigate the emotional complexities of forgiveness, providing reassurance and guidance along the way. With this encouragement, they are better able to release their anger and move toward forgiveness.

18

True Versus Junk Values

Charlotte heard her name being called repeatedly, accompanied by a gentle shaking of her arm. Despite the strong urge to respond, she struggled to open her eyes. The shaking grew more insistent, and the voice became louder, finally coaxing her awake. She made an effort to cooperate by whispering a faint "yes" but still found it challenging to lift her eyelids. As the voice reassured her that she was out of surgery and in the recovery room, Charlotte began to process this information. Slowly, she managed to open her eyes, greeted by the sight of a blonde nurse leaning over her with a concerned expression. With great effort, Charlotte attempted to ask for water. The masked nurse nodded understandingly, reaching for a glass with a straw and offering it to Charlotte.

Guiding Charlotte to take small sips, the nurse began to explain that Charlotte had been under anesthesia for longer than anticipated, which could lead to a reaction. The nurse then mentioned that Charlotte's friend was waiting downstairs with a ride home and that she would assist in getting her dressed and accompany her to the car. Charlotte had decided against staying at the recovery center as per her surgeon's advice, signing a release to allow her friend to pick her up and stay with her overnight.

Feeling weaker than expected, Charlotte complied with the nurse's directions, albeit with pauses and delayed responses. The nurse guided her down in a wheelchair and helped her into her friend's car while providing instructions for her overnight care, including managing the drains. Charlotte then noticed the drains on her left side for the first time, prompting her to ask what had happened during the surgery. The surgeon hadn't visited her afterward, or she had been unconscious if he had. The uncertainty was disconcerting. The nurse would only say that the doctor would call her tomorrow.

That night was marked by intense pain, discomfort, and frequent bouts of vomiting, a common reaction Charlotte experienced after anesthesia. Despite these challenges, she persevered. The next day, she finally had the opportunity to meet with her surgeon, who explained her condition. Charlotte had accumulated a significant amount of scar tissue from the impact of the accident, necessitating its removal and subsequent reconstructive procedures.

Charlotte left the appointment with relief, feeling that she could now leave this chapter behind and move forward. However, a thought lingered: Could her psyche also bear scars, much like the buildup of scar tissue from life's endured traumas? She contemplated this parallel between the body's formation of scar tissue and the psyche's creation of protective mechanisms. Just as scar tissue acts as a barrier to protect the body, the psyche may build emotional walls as a defense mechanism in response to trauma. These protective mechanisms can manifest as psychological barriers or coping strategies that shield the individual from further harm. In essence, the mind's reaction to trauma is to fortify itself by developing additional protective layers, similar to how the body naturally responds to physical injury.

The challenge lies in the fact that, much like the body, the mind can sometimes overbuild its protective mechanisms, which can lead to more harm than good. Unlike the relatively straightforward process of removing residual buildup from the body with the help of a skilled surgeon, addressing these psychological barriers is significantly more complex. To begin with, it requires an exceptionally aware individual to recognize the presence of these emotional walls or residual buildup in the psyche. Once they are identified, it takes a courageous soul to be willing to lower these barriers, despite the lingering threats and fears associated with vulnerability. Moreover, sustaining this process of dismantling psychological defenses demands an audacious personality—someone who can persevere in the face of imminent dangers and uncertainties that arise from exposing oneself emotionally. In essence, while repairing physical scars may require surgical expertise, dismantling emotional barriers necessitates a deep level of self-awareness, courage, and resilience.

Charlotte smiled as she imagined the next phase of her personal growth journey. While it had been challenging to address the physical damage from her accident, she acknowledged that healing from the emotional wounds was an even more formidable task. However, she found solace in the symbolism of her journey, viewing it as a transformative process akin to the healing of physical scars but on a deeper emotional level. This perspective provided her with a more helpful image for navigating her healing journey and embracing the growth that comes with it.

The following weeks were a whirlwind of doctors' appointments and recovery tasks, all of which Charlotte managed with the support of her sister and friends. Each passing day brought renewed strength, both physically and emotionally. Adam had sent her flowers after the surgery and tried to reach out to her multiple times, yet Charlotte chose to leave his calls and messages unanswered. She felt no inclination to engage with him further, fully aware of the complexities of their relationship.

Despite her resolve, Charlotte couldn't shake a nagging question: Why had Adam resurfaced after all this time, especially given that he was already in another relationship? This question added to her emotional burden, but she focused on her own healing and well-being. Deep down, she realized that no justification from Adam would truly alleviate her pain or change the outcome.

Her struggle with moving forward troubled her. She questioned how much her difficulty in letting go stemmed from her own traumatic experiences. She reflected on whether her emotional attachment to Adam was tied to the sudden and painful disruption of her bond with her father, where she was thrust into a harsh reality without closure or farewell. Was it possible that her desire to maintain control in her relationship with Adam was a subconscious attempt to compensate for the control she had lost in that earlier chapter of her life? She granted herself the space to delve deeper into the connection between these two losses.

Ultimately, regardless of how they occur, all losses carry the same hollow ache. The pain felt identical in both cases; the distinction lay in one person (her father) being forcibly taken from her, while the other (Adam) chose to depart, possibly carrying a component of rejection that amplified the hurt. The thought that losing Adam had inflicted deeper emotional wounds than losing her father caused Charlotte to feel intense feelings of shame and guilt. How could she even dare to compare the two? The reality was, despite her conflicting emotions, losing a partner always seems to inflict a more piercing agony on an adult than losing a parent. Regardless of how or why, they were both gone. She had to find a way to navigate life without either of these men.

One thing that became abundantly clear was that holding on for the sake of external gratification came at the expense of her values, and Charlotte knew all too well that without her values, she would crumble. As enticing as that gratification might be, it would only feel right and meaningful if it aligned with her value system. The moment it caused her to stray from that alignment, it would begin to erode her sense of self, leading to more harm than benefit.

Every fiber of her being hinted at embracing the next phase, a sensation deeply rooted in personal growth. Her emotions had harmonized with her rationality, and she had sincerely lost interest in any toxic dynamics. On the contrary, she yearned for stability, reliability, and openness, firmly convinced that she deserved nothing short of these qualities. She was determined not to compromise on these standards.

Charlotte was driving back from a yoga class, the rhythmic hum of her car blending with the calming echoes of her practice. Amid the serenity, she was seized by a sudden craving for yellowtail carpaccio. As she turn off the main boulevard toward that delicious desire, her phone interrupted. The car's automated voice announced, "Tarek calling." Without hesitation, Charlotte pressed the green answer button, the carpaccio momentarily postponed.

Tarek's voice resonated through the phone, asking if she would join him for dinner. Charlotte, her mind still lingering on the flavors of sushi, explained her specific craving. To her delight, Tarek revealed his familiarity with the restaurant she had in mind. He would make a reservation and pick her up in an hour.

As the call ended, Charlotte's excitement grew—though she wasn't certain whether this heightened emotion was because of Tarek or the yellowtail. Little did she know that this evening would mark the beginning of a whole new chapter for her—filled with surprises.

Are You Pursuing True Purpose or Merely Getting Lost in Distractions?

In *Lost Connections*, researcher Johann Hari explores the distinction between meaningful and junk values, linking mental health challenges to disconnections from the former and attachments to the latter.[9] He defines junk values as those centered around material wealth, status, and appearance, which often lead to an emptiness and a disconnection. According to Hari, people's dissatisfaction is largely a result of these associations. On the contrary, authentic values that contribute to fulfillment and well-being are rooted in connections with others, nature, autonomy, meaningful work, and a commitment to social justice and fairness. Hari highlights how the disconnect from true values and the prevalence of junk values in modern society contribute to rising rates of depression, anxiety, and other mental health disorders. He argues that addressing the underlying societal factors promoting junk values and prioritizing true values can be transformative in addressing the root causes of mental health challenges.

The connection between societal values and our true value system is a complex and often challenging aspect of human experience. As members of society, we are inevitably influenced by societal values and norms from an early age. These values are communicated through various channels, including family, education, media, and cultural institutions. We receive messages about what success looks like, how we should present ourselves,

9 Johann Hari, *Lost Connections: Uncovering the Real Causes of Depression—and the Unexpected Solutions* (Bloomsbury, 2018).

and what is deemed socially valuable. These societal influences can shape our beliefs, behaviors, and aspirations, sometimes leading us away from our true value system. It's practically impossible to escape the influence of societal norms due to the pervasive nature of socialization processes that begin in childhood and continue throughout our lives.

In such a landscape, it becomes crucial to cultivate self-awareness, critical thinking, and resilience against these external influences that are not aligned with our values. By questioning the motives behind societal messages, evaluating their alignment with our authentic values, and consciously choosing how we engage with them, we can create a space for our true values to thrive. The questions that arise are these: To what extent do these societal influences genuinely reflect our own values, and how fulfilled do we feel when we conform to them?

Throughout our lives, we strive to strike a delicate balance between societal expectations and our authentic values. At times, we may find ourselves conforming to certain standards or adopting behaviors that align with societal norms, even if they don't fully resonate with our true selves. This adaptation to societal values can occur subconsciously and gradually, influenced by social pressure, fear of judgment, or a desire for acceptance and validation.

As we chase these illusory benchmarks, we unwittingly choose misguided paths, pursuing careers and relationships that align with what we think we want. This erroneous conviction sets the stage for a misalignment of our true desires and aspirations. Consequently, many people find themselves grappling with a profound discontentment, paving the way for what is commonly known as a mislived life crisis.

Despite achieving traditional markers of success, individuals feel profoundly unfulfilled, questioning the purpose of their work, their relationships, and even their sense of self. Such a crisis often leads to a painful but necessary period of self-reflection, where they may begin to ask: *What do I truly want? What makes me feel alive?*

This realization can act as a catalyst for transformation, prompting individuals to confront the dissonance between their current lives and their inner values. For some, it may mean leaving a secure career to pursue a passion that resonates more deeply with who they are, or reevaluating relationships to prioritize connections that are rooted in authenticity and mutual respect. Others may shift their lifestyles, carving out time for creative pursuits, meaningful volunteer work, or new learning experiences that align with their true aspirations.

Ultimately, the journey from this crisis to a more fulfilling life requires courage and self-honesty. By realigning their lives with values that genuinely resonate, individuals can move beyond the illusion of success and toward a life that offers a deeper sense of purpose and satisfaction.

Core Values Versus Junk Values

Contrary to the success-failure dichotomy of junk values, core values operate on a different plane. They are not contingent on specific achievements or the avoidance of failure. Instead, they are deeply rooted in our ability to connect with ourselves and with others. By embracing core values, we embark on a journey that transcends the narrow confines of success and failure, offering a more fulfilling and resilient framework for navigating life.

The impact of chasing junk values goes beyond career choices, seeping into the essence of our relationships. In the intricate dance of human connections, we often find ourselves ensnared in the chase for the wrong relationships—connections that match external markers of success or societal norms rather than genuine compatibility. This misguided approach, reminiscent of pursuing a mismatched career, lays the groundwork for relational disharmony. It is a profound challenge when we discover that our desires are misaligned with our true selves.

We may earnestly believe that what we pursue is what we genuinely want, only to realize later that our aspirations were misguided. Instead of allowing our authentic needs and desires to naturally manifest, we doggedly pursue what we have misconstrued as our needs. This misguided pursuit often leads to emptiness and dissatisfaction, particularly in relationships. We may find ourselves in partnerships that lack genuine harmony, leading to loneliness and unhappiness. It's common for people in such situations to erroneously blame their partners for their discontent, when in reality, the root cause lies in their own misconceptions about themselves and their true desires.

For instance, imagine someone who grows up believing that success in a relationship is defined by material markers, like a partner's career status or social standing. Driven by this belief, they may pursue relationships with individuals who appear successful on the surface but lack the emotional connection or shared values that truly matter to them. Over time, they find themselves feeling unfulfilled, even lonely, despite their partner meeting those external "criteria" of success.

This disillusionment highlights how pursuing relationships based on external ideals, or junk values, can lead to a crisis point. When we cultivate relationships rooted in societal expectations rather than authentic connection, we may face profound relational anguish. This dissonance between what we believed would bring happiness and the reality of unmet emotional needs reveals the importance of aligning our relationships with our true values, rather than simply fulfilling immediate desires or needs that may not reflect our deepest values. Choosing to pursue connections that resonate with our authentic selves creates a more enduring and fulfilling foundation for relationship satisfaction.

Just as in the other realms, the pursuit of junk values in relationships can lead to a crisis point. We may discover that the relationships we've cultivated, based on external ideals rather than genuine connection, fail to provide the fulfillment we crave. Alternatively, the dissonance between reality and unmet expectations can sow the seeds of profound relational anguish.

Embracing core values in both career and relationships paves the way for a more holistic and fulfilling life, offering resilience in the face of the crises that often accompany the pursuit of illusory ideals. As we navigate the intricate terrain of life, understanding the distinction between junk values and core values becomes paramount. Shifting our focus from the transient allure of success and failure, we can discover a more meaningful and purposeful existence. To embark on the journey of discovering this realm, we must summon the courage to release the pretense of what we have been conditioned to label as a successful life.

In embarking on this journey, we may feel estranged from a community that upholds the false values we've let go of. This underscores the paramount importance of cultivating profound self-awareness and unwavering courage. To attain our optimal state of functioning, we must endure the discomfort of establishing our own rhythm and liberating ourselves from societal dictates.

Clarifying Core Values and Living with Purpose

Core values are the guiding principles that shape your most important life decisions. These values often reflect what truly matters to you on a deep, personal level and are consistent across various aspects of your life. By aligning your decisions with these core values, you create a sense of fulfillment and authenticity. Imagine someone who values integrity above all else. When faced with a challenging situation at work, they choose to be honest with their team, even if it means facing short-term difficulties. This decision aligns with their core value of honesty, and although the situation is tough, they feel a sense of peace knowing they've acted in accordance with their beliefs.

Living according to your core values often creates a sense of harmony between your actions and your beliefs. When your values and choices are in sync, you experience greater fulfillment, and life feels more meaningful. This alignment allows you to move through life with confidence and clarity. Someone who deeply values personal growth invests time in activities that challenge and expand their mind, such as learning new skills or pursuing creative projects. By aligning their actions with their core value of growth, they feel a sense of fulfillment and purpose, which enhances their overall well-being.

Junk values, on the other hand, are often imposed by societal expectations or external influences, rather than arising from within. These values may lead you to chase goals that feel hollow or unfulfilling in the long run. Identifying these superficial values helps you avoid the trap of living by standards that don't truly resonate with your inner self. Consider someone who is focused on achieving a high social status or wealth because society equates success with material accumulation. However, after reaching their financial goals, they realize that the pursuit of status has left them feeling empty and disconnected from what actually brings them joy. Recognizing that these values were never core to their identity, they begin to shift their focus toward relationships and meaningful experiences, which provide deeper satisfaction.

Your core values act as anchors during times of adversity. When you face difficult circumstances, values such as resilience, empathy, or perseverance can guide you through the storm and provide clarity in decision-making. Core values offer stability and direction when everything else feels uncertain. In the midst of a personal crisis, someone whose core value is family decides to prioritize spending time with loved ones over career advancement. This decision not only helps them navigate the emotional challenges they face but also reinforces their commitment to their family, which brings a sense of stability and support during a difficult time.

Core values are deeply personal, whereas junk values are often adopted unconsciously through societal pressure, peer influence, or media exposure. By reflecting on the origin of your values, you can distinguish between those that truly reflect who you are and those that have been imposed on you. Someone might feel pressure to pursue a high-powered career because it's seen as the "right" path for success in their social circle. However, upon introspection, they realize their true passion lies in working with non-profit organizations and making a direct impact on their community. Recognizing that the pursuit of status is a junk value for them, they choose to align their career with their core value of service.

As you grow and evolve, some values that once seemed important may no longer serve your well-being or personal growth. Recognizing when it's time to release these outdated values allows you to create space for values that better align with your current life stage and goals. A person who used to value recognition and validation from others might realize that constantly seeking approval has led them to compromise their authenticity. They decide to let go of the need for external validation and instead embrace self-acceptance and independence as core values. This shift allows them to experience greater freedom and confidence in their personal and professional life.

A key characteristic of core values is their consistency across different areas of life, whether in relationships, work, or personal growth. When your values are consistent, they provide a clear sense of purpose and coherence, helping you make decisions that feel authentic across all aspects of your life. Someone whose core value is kindness shows the same level of care and respect in their personal relationships as they do in their professional life. Whether they are supporting a friend in need or helping a colleague solve a problem, their consistent application of kindness reflects a deep commitment to living in alignment with their core values.

When you are rooted in your core values, decision-making becomes easier and more confident. Rather than being swayed by temporary emotions or external pressures, your core values guide you toward choices that reflect your true self and long-term goals. Faced with a tempting but ethically questionable business opportunity, someone who values integrity decides to decline, despite the potential financial gain. Their clear commitment to honesty gives them confidence in their decision, knowing they are staying true to their principles and avoiding choices that would lead to internal conflict.

Core values are those that bring you a deep sense of fulfillment and meaning. Unlike junk values, which often leave you feeling unfulfilled, core values are aligned with your true desires and aspirations, leading to a richer and more rewarding life. After years of pursuing wealth and recognition, someone realizes that their greatest source of happiness comes from creativity and self-expression. They decide to dedicate more time to writing and art, even if it means earning less money. By aligning their life with their core value of creativity, they experience a deeper sense of purpose and fulfillment.

Surrounding yourself with people and environments that reflect your core values helps you stay committed to living in alignment with what matters most. A supportive environment reinforces your dedication to those values and helps you maintain focus, even when external pressures arise. A person who values personal growth and mindfulness actively seeks out relationships with others who share those values. They create a social circle where growth, curiosity, and self-awareness are celebrated. This supportive environment helps them stay grounded and aligned with their values, making it easier to continue their journey of self-development.

19

Association Versus Dissociation

Back in Los Angeles, in the enchanting ambiance of her favorite hotel lobby, Charlotte found herself seated across from Tarek, a fireplace casting a warm glow. The elegant strains of a piano filled the air, a gentle rendition of "White Christmas." As Tarek responded to an email, Charlotte observed the play of firelight on his features, contemplating the events of the past three months.

Tarek exuded a calm yet strong presence that defied intimidation. Charlotte, accustomed to perceiving him as more gentle than imposing, often questioned her true feelings. However, in this moment, something shifted. Tarek's gentleness became remarkably soothing and attractive, unveiling a depth that Charlotte hadn't fully recognized before. She felt secure and protected in his presence.

As the piano seamlessly transitioned into an upbeat melody, the crowd in the lobby began to gather for an impromptu dance. Tarek, captivated by the festive atmosphere, remarked, "I love the holiday season; it makes everyone so joyful." Charlotte couldn't help but smile. Tarek rose, extending a hand, which she wordlessly took.

Charlotte allowed herself to be led into the dance. Resting her head on Tarek's shoulder, she absorbed the serenity of the moment. The piano's melody intertwined with the joyous laughter and movement of the crowd, creating a harmonious symphony of shared experiences. Under the spell of the holiday spirit, Charlotte discovered an appreciation for the depth and warmth that Tarek brought into her life.

She nestled in Tarek's embrace, absorbing the warmth and serenity of the moment. When he eventually pulled back, concern was etched on his features. He asked if she was all right. Charlotte, attempting to conceal her reflections, responded with a casual assurance, "Couldn't be any better."

However, Tarek, perceptive to the subtle shifts in her demeanor, persisted. "You seem like you are somewhere else. Is something bothering you?"

Uncomfortable with the directness of the question, Charlotte averted her gaze, seeking refuge from the vulnerability of the moment. Swiftly, she walked toward her coat, the act a subtle escape from the discomfort of the inquiry, and remarked, "If we don't hurry, we'll be late for dinner." Tarek followed.

Charlotte found herself repeatedly navigating the depths of

her internal conflict, grappling with the tension between the allure of what captivated her and the deeper desires of her authentic self. She recognized the pull toward men like Adam—those who embodied danger and excitement, but whose unpredictability left her vulnerable to emotional harm. It was a pattern, almost a psychological blueprint, rooted in the thrill of uncertainty and the heightened emotional arousal that came with it. But she was also aware that this attraction was a manifestation of unresolved elements within her, a compulsion that kept her bound to familiar cycles of excitement and disappointment.

With Tarek, on the other hand, she experienced something entirely different. His steady, reliable presence offered her a sense of peace, security, and emotional stability. But in that safety, she also felt a subtle undercurrent of disinterest, which was her mistaking the absence of emotional chaos for boredom. Psychologically, she understood that this reaction stemmed from her internalization of love as something volatile and consuming, rather than calm and grounding. Her attraction to Adam's unpredictability was not just about preference; it was a reflection of deep, unresolved emotional patterns.

In Tarek's predictability, Charlotte faced a quieter struggle—the discomfort of redefining love not as an exhilarating high but as a grounded, nurturing force. And while she intellectually understood the value of such a connection, emotionally she was still reconciling the gap between what she had been conditioned to crave and what she now knew was essential for her emotional growth and well-being.

The tension between the familiar but harmful and the unfamiliar but healthy represented a fundamental shift in her understanding of intimacy, which required her to unlearn patterns deeply ingrained in her psyche. Despite years of therapy and reflection, she couldn't escape the magnetic pull of the narcissist. She was aware enough to avoid being fully ensnared by it, recognizing its potential toxicity, but it drew her all the same.

At the restaurant, Tarek sat across the table, maintaining an assertive gaze. Charlotte averted her eyes, fully aware that he was silently prompting her to speak about her feelings. Tarek had made it clear that he would not be in a relationship with a woman who was not fully present. Charlotte was struck by the lack of aggression when he said this, and how he navigated the conversation with calm, gentleness, and sophistication. She knew she was testing this conviction now.

He extended his hand across the table, and she hesitantly reached out to take it. The warmth of his touch enveloped her, prompting her to close her eyes. A single tear escaped, carrying with it a surge of emotions she had been trying to ignore.

He gently wiped it from her face, taking her hand to his cheek and kissing it. His voice, surprisingly steady, caught her off guard. "Charlotte," he began, "the past three months have been a fortunate journey for us. But much of my pleasure comes from knowing I can bring you joy. When I see you detached or sad, I can't help but wonder about the cause of that pain. I would hate to be the source of it."

Charlotte once again averted her gaze. She deeply respected

him, valuing his honesty and directness. However, she found herself unable to fully reveal herself. She grasped both of his hands with hers, as if to anchor herself to the present moment, a lifeline to prevent herself from disappearing into the tumult of her thoughts. Then, she deliberately locked eyes with him. As she began to speak, she was enveloped by a feeling of power and presence.

She thanked him for the time they had shared so far, highlighting how rewarding and healing the experience had been. Her current lack of joy had nothing to do with him, she said, but was intricately tied to her ongoing internal battles. She implored him to be patient, assuring him that, given time, she would navigate through.

The next day, Charlotte found herself bundled up on a chaise longue in her analyst's office, unraveling how her inner struggle was once again wreaking havoc on her life, this time disrupting a potentially significant relationship.

The analyst looked up at her and asked, "Why do you care?"

Charlotte, intrigued, met her gaze.

The analyst continued, "Over the years, many wonderful men like Tarek have entered your life, ready to offer everything—marriage, family, and love. You've said no to every one of them and allowed someone like Adam to treat you the way he did for as long as he did. Tarek is just one of those men. Why does it matter if, once again, you walk away from something good? Apparently, you prefer Adam." Her tone was firm, devoid of the usual empathy, and Charlotte felt a level of judgment she had never experienced before. However, what stung the most was the undeniable truth embedded in the analyst's statement.

Charlotte sat back. She understood that these words needed to resonate within her, leaving an indelible mark that would prompt a different course of action. In response, she could only muster, "You are right. I have constructed my life based on my preferences rather than reality. Perhaps, just perhaps, it's time for me to stop being a spoiled brat."

The analyst, with a slight grin, continued, "You are not a spoiled brat; on the contrary, you are a very responsible adult. As such, you must make decisions that support that."

Charlotte found herself feeling a mixture of fascination and discomfort. The potential for a significant shift in perspective intrigued her, promising a profound transformation. But underlying this fascination was a sense of unease from sacrificing her own happiness. Despite wanting this fresh insight, she grappled with feeling inadequate and doubted herself. With a blend of apprehension and determination, Charlotte made a solemn vow to anchor herself firmly in the present moment. She realized that her ability to stay grounded faltered when she allowed herself to be consumed by thoughts of the past.

This newfound awareness empowered Charlotte to cultivate mindfulness, liberating herself from the burdens of hindsight. With each deliberate breath, she reclaimed control over her thoughts, steering them away from the past. In the tranquility of the present, she discovered a sanctuary where doubts and insecurities held no sway.

Why Do You Feel Disconnected from Reality?

Dissociation manifests as a disruption in the seamless integration of consciousness, memory, identity, and perception. A nuanced examination of dissociation in relation to reality reveals it as a distinct form of detachment, contrasting with the fabrication of false realities seen in psychosis.

Diverse perspectives have surfaced, framing dissociation within a spectrum: At one end, dissociation functions as a coping mechanism against monotony and stress, often materializing as benign daydreaming. At the opposite end, it can manifest as a pathological condition, characterized by derealization or even profound amnesia. Within this spectrum, the term *dissociation* encompasses a wide range of experiences, spanning from fleeting moments of mental escape to the complexities of severe disorders like dissociative identity disorder.

Understanding the triggers and causes of dissociation is crucial for effective therapeutic interventions. This knowledge unveils the adaptive functions and coping mechanisms inherent in dissociation, offering a compass for those navigating overwhelming circumstances on their journey toward healing.

Associations denote the mental connections between different aspects of consciousness, memory, and identity. Dissociation, on the other hand, disrupts these normal associations, leading to a disjunction between thoughts, emotions, or elements of one's identity. Normally, associations contribute to a cohesive and integrated sense of self and reality. However, in dissociation, these associations become fragmented or disrupted, resulting in altered states of consciousness. For instance, traumatic memories may be dissociated or separated from an individual's everyday awareness, engendering a sense of detachment.

Understanding associations in the context of dissociation proves crucial for therapists and mental health professionals working to address and integrate dissociated aspects, fostering a more coherent and unified sense of self for those of us experiencing dissociative symptoms. Therapeutic interventions often aim to reestablish healthy associations and connections within our mental processes. To address dislocation—which refers to the feeling of being disconnected from one's surroundings, body, or sense of self—our initial steps must focus on enhancing mental wellness and promoting adaptive coping strategies. This may involve grounding techniques, mindfulness practices, and strengthening emotional regulation to support a stable foundation for further therapeutic work.

During a traumatic event, we often form negative associations between the traumatic experience and otherwise neutral objects. For example, someone who has suffered a car accident may subsequently associate cars with fear or physiological distress. A significant component of trauma therapy involves the deliberate process of reversing these negative associations and restoring the neutrality to these triggers. This therapeutic approach aims to neutralize heightened emotional responses tied to specific objects, empowering us to regain control and alleviate the emotional distress linked to traumatic memories. Through targeted interventions and strategic techniques, therapists collaborate with their patients to reshape their perceptions and reactions, ultimately fostering a healthier and more adaptive relationship with elements that were previously triggering.

This therapeutic approach serves the additional purpose of preventing the patient from further dissociation, which often emerges as a coping mechanism in response to the experienced pain. By addressing and neutralizing the negative associations linked to traumatic memories, therapists work to create a protective buffer against the tendency to dissociate. This aims to help the patient stay more connected to their present reality and emotions, promoting a healthier and more integrated response to past trauma.

Dissociation, in its everyday manifestation, plays a vital role as an internal mechanism facilitating mental respite and aiding in the regulation of cognitive input. However, our current discourse homes in on the intricacies of trauma-induced dissociation, characterized by the spontaneous takeover of consciousness by unresolved emotional states. Extended engagement in this maladaptive form of dissociation can result in disengagement not only from the factual aspects of their lives but also from the essential resources required to pursue and accomplish their objectives. Through reassociation, we can construct an environment that fosters a more integrated perspective of their reality, as opposed to a fragmented one.

Restoring Connection Through Grounded Presence

Dissociation often emerges as a protective mechanism in response to overwhelming or traumatic experiences, creating a sense of emotional or mental detachment from reality. Moving from dissociation toward association involves identifying the specific triggers and patterns that lead to this state and developing strategies to remain grounded and present.

The following are key ways to reframe dissociation and deepen your understanding of its impact on your experiences.

- Recognize the trigger that leads to dissociation.

  Dissociation often stems from specific memories or experiences that elicit feelings of detachment. Identifying these triggers allows you to understand how and when dissociation occurs, which is the first step in reframing your response.

- Practice grounding techniques when you feel out of control.

  Recognize when feelings of being out of control trigger dissociation and prepare with grounding techniques, such as deep breathing or focusing on your surroundings. This awareness allows you to stay connected in similar situations by using grounding tools proactively.

- Identify sensory triggers that may lead to dissociation.

  Certain smells, sounds, or textures can unconsciously evoke memories tied to dissociation. For example, if the smell of a particular perfume reminds you of a distressing experience, recognizing this connection allows you to either avoid the trigger or use mindfulness techniques to create new, positive associations.

- Acknowledge individuals or relationships that may act as dissociative triggers.

  Some people or interactions may unintentionally trigger dissociation, particularly if they're connected to past trauma. Recognizing these interactions allows you to protect your emotional space. For example, if you dissociate around a family member who reminds you of unresolved trauma, setting boundaries or using grounding techniques beforehand can reduce the dissociative response.

- Understand how unresolved emotions and trauma contribute to dissociation.

  Dissociative episodes are often linked to unprocessed emotions. Understanding the role of past trauma allows you to begin healing and reduce automatic dissociative responses. For instance, if shouting evokes memories of childhood trauma, working through these emotions in therapy can lessen the link between shouting and dissociation.

- Reflect on cultural or societal influences on your coping mechanisms.

  Dissociation may develop as a coping mechanism in cultures that discourage emotional expression. Recognizing these societal influences allows you to unlearn unhealthy emotional responses. In a culture where vulnerability is seen as weakness, acknowledging this influence enables you to consciously adopt healthier coping strategies.

- Reflect on how dissociation affects daily functioning and relationships.

  Dissociation can impact tasks, relationships, and communication. Recognizing when it affects your performance helps you develop strategies to stay engaged. For instance, if you dissociate during work meetings, use grounding techniques like deep breaths or a stress ball to help maintain focus.

- Observe the physical signs of dissociation in your body.

  Dissociation often includes physical responses, like numbness or shallow breathing. Noticing these signals early allows you to counteract dissociation with grounding techniques, like pressing your feet firmly on the ground or holding something cold to reengage with the present.

- Notice cognitive shifts that accompany dissociation.

  Dissociative episodes can cause fragmented thoughts or a distorted sense of time. Becoming aware of these mental shifts allows you to manage them by practicing mental grounding, such as naming objects in the room to reanchor your thoughts.

- Seek professional support to explore dissociation more deeply.

  Discussing dissociation with a therapist provides insight into patterns and triggers, helping to reduce the frequency and intensity of dissociative episodes. Therapy techniques like Eye Movement Desensitization and

Reprocessing (EMDR) or Cognitive Behavioral Therapy (CBT) can help you process trauma and create healthier coping mechanisms.

Developing an awareness of dissociation and its triggers is a powerful step toward reclaiming control over your experiences. By practicing these strategies, you build a tool kit for staying grounded and connected, even in challenging situations. Remember that this process is gradual; cultivating resilience and self-understanding takes time and patience. With the support of these practices—and, if needed, guidance from a mental health professional—you can navigate dissociative episodes more effectively, fostering a sense of coherence and integration within yourself. This journey of self-awareness ultimately empowers you to engage more fully with life, equipped with the tools to face each moment authentically.

20

Life Versus Death

Charlotte ducked into a coffee shop, seeking refuge from the sudden rain that had interrupted her Sunday morning errands. Fresh from the salon with her hair styled for the upcoming anniversary dinner with Tarek, she was determined not to let the weather dampen her spirits or her perfectly coiffed hair. Their anniversary reignited a sense of delight within her, and she marveled at how quickly a year had passed since they first embarked on their relationship.

As she approached the counter, Charlotte ordered an almond cappuccino to justify her stay, even though she had already indulged in her morning coffee. Clutching a card intended for Tarek later that evening, she hoped that the reflections on their experiences together would inspire the perfect words to convey her emotions.

Seated by the window, Charlotte found joy in observing the bustling street outside. Her mind wandered back to her first meeting with Tarek in London and the subsequent chapters of their relationship. The past year had unfolded with a gradual deepening of intimacy and love between them. They shared a harmonious balance and a foundation of transparency. While they faced the typical relationship challenges and fluctuations, those were minor compared with her past experiences. In Tarek's presence, she felt a profound sense of security—true emotional safety.

But amid this sense of comfort, doubts crept in. Was Tarek simply a safe haven she chose over genuine love? Her ongoing emotional battle raised questions about the authenticity of their harmony and whether it stemmed from love, unlike the pain-laden love she had known before. What if this stability represented genuine, healthy love, and her past experiences were merely a painful misunderstanding of it? Each turn of the metaphorical pages of her heart revealed the delicate and uncertain dance between comfort and the elusive true love. She was lost in her thoughts, gradually putting her pen to paper to write his card when she felt a shadow cast over her paper. She looked up, and sure enough, there he was, just when she was finally moving on and done with his nonsense.

Adam appeared unchanged except for a hint of gray around his temples. If she were honest with herself, the aging process only rendered him more maturely attractive. She braced for the customary plummet of her heart, the rapid beating, the surge in her body temperature, almost as if she were preparing herself for the ritual. However, this time nothing happened. She relished the rare feeling of having the upper hand and remained remarkably still. Was it possible that he had lost his allure in her eyes, or had she, at last, outgrown his behavior?

"The rain is coming down pretty hard out there," Adam said.

She nodded—no pleasantries; there was nothing more to be said by either of them. The magic was gone, replaced only by a potentially healed wound that masochistically felt good to touch but that she knew intellectually was better left untouched.

Clarity washed over her. Perhaps love is intricately woven into the fabric of our psychology, drawing us toward those with similar emotional maturity levels. At one juncture, Adam had been the embodiment of her attraction, a dynamic that inadvertently triggered responses tied to her trauma. However, she had now outgrown this pattern. His offerings were no longer alluring; she had evolved. Her love for Adam had been genuine at the time, but she no longer found herself drawn to him. She smiled.

Completely oblivious to her introspective journey, Adam greeted the smile warmly and murmured, "I thought I'd never see you smile again."

The irony didn't escape her; she found it intriguing. She was smiling as a result of overcoming her obsession with him, while he, true to his narcissistic tendencies, attributed the smile to himself. Her grin widened when she made that connection, but there was no need to correct him. The person she needed to confront was herself, and it seemed like she had finally achieved that after enduring much pain and suffering.

Adam leaned forward, placing his hand on her shoulder, and charmingly uttered, "Char, I am trying to figure things out. You can't fault me for that."

She casually shrugged to dislodge his hand from her shoulder and replied, "You are right. You are trying, and I can't fault you for that. But I can fault myself for being okay with your confusion for so long."

He eased into the chair across from her, apparently hoping to weave the threads of their conversation further. In response, she gracefully rose, collected her belongings, and left.

As the rain intensified, she stepped out into the very element she once sought shelter from. The concern for her hair vanished, replaced by a profound sense of liberation—free from him, free from the labyrinth of inner demons, and emancipated from yielding her happiness to a chapter that no longer served her.

In the downpour, she felt the cleansing touch of raindrops, a poetic baptism washing away the stains of the past. Excitement for the unwritten chapters of the future surged within her, and clarity radiated about the path she was destined to tread. It required her to bid farewell to a part of herself, a departure accompanied by a fierce internal struggle, as is often the case. Just like losing someone you dearly cherish, letting go of facets of yourself is a painful odyssey.

Charlotte understood that she held both healthy and unhealthy fragments within herself. The robust dynamics of her healthier aspects propelled her toward fulfillment and the realization of her desires, while the powerful grip of her unhealthy facets occasionally shackled her, dragging her into a darkness she yearned to escape but struggled to navigate. The only pathway out demanded gradually disowning the unwholesome, with hopes of replacing it with the robust and healthy.

It's always a challenge to release a part of yourself, to create space for something new. A stubborn inclination persists, yearning to cling to the familiar—as the saying goes, "Better the devil we know than the devil we don't." She embraced the transformative dance, acknowledging that within the surrender lies the birth of a brighter and more authentic self.

Perhaps that's why the journey felt arduous all this time—viewing it through the lens of mere death and not realizing it was a profound rebirth. It wasn't just the burial of a part of herself; it was a celebration of the emergence of something new. Her musings lingered on the parallels between this rebirth and the loss of her father, a pivotal point in her existence. Could his passing, too, be a rebirth—not just of his soul but also of her life after his departure?

She had to master the art of living and surviving without his protective care, a transformative process akin to a rebirth. Her dependent side had to fade, creating space for a more independent survivor. This journey, though exquisitely painful, was one she had endured—a challenging path that ultimately led to a deeply liberating transformation.

She strolled from the coffee shop to her car, gracefully sank into the seat, her rain-soaked attire and once flawless hair now cascading over the seat. From the shelter of her car, she watched the last drops of rain pirouette on her windshield. The sun emerged from its celestial curtain, casting rays that gently unveiled a rainbow, a divine brushstroke working its way through the sky. It was the sign she sought, a harmonious convergence of all the emotions woven into the fabric of the past hour—doubts, pain, resolution, and the profound meaning beneath it all.

In the quiet sanctuary of her car, she recognized that, much like nature, every moment holds something new for us. We interpret it sometimes as positive, like the warm embrace of sunshine, and at other times as negative, mirroring the melancholy dance of raindrops. Each possesses its own merit, and neither exists without the other.

She knew that while things might make sense in the present moment, tomorrow would likely bring its own set of confusions, doubts, and an unfamiliar pain she hadn't yet learned to navigate. Torn between ups and downs, she was certain that, just as she had with this current chapter, she would find her way through the next.

Charlotte reached into her bag and retrieved the card for Tarek. With a sense of purpose, she began to write, her emotions flowing onto the paper. She no longer had to ponder how to express herself or what to say; the words flowed effortlessly from her pen, as if they had been waiting to be released.

Beloved Tarek,

In your embrace, I've learned the softness of love's touch,

Where pain is but a distant echo, and hearts intertwine as such.

You've led me to discover the beauty within,

Guiding me to my essence, where true virtues begin.

Grateful am I for your gentle guiding light,

For in your love's embrace, I find my might.
May I mirror your grace, half as divine,
As you've painted my world with hues so delight.

Forever yours,

Charlotte

She started the car and drove back to her apartment. She directed her thoughts toward the future, gradually leaving the shadows of the past behind. The imprint of her father's memory remained etched in her heart, just as the intense emotions shared with Adam lingered vividly in her soul. She carried fragments of them both, intricately woven into the fabric of her essence. Their collective experiences molded the person she had become, a synthesis of their shared joys and sorrows.

What distinguished her from her past was the acknowledgment of pain not as an adversary but as an inseparable part of her narrative. Amid the echoes of past challenges, she embraced the lessons learned, navigating a course forward. Each lesson exacted its toll, and for her, the price was paid in the currency of pain; but she accepted this with grace, recognizing that the symphony of her existence includes both the harmonious chords of joy and the poignant notes of suffering.

How Can You Make Peace with Life's End?

Life and death define the essence of being human. Life unfolds as a vibrant tapestry interwoven with moments of joy and pain—a journey enriched by laughter, tears, and the intricate dance of emotions. Death stands as the inescapable denouement, veiled in mystery and often evoking contemplation.

Life is transient, marked by the relentless passage of time and the pursuit of purpose. It encompasses the breaths we take, the connections we forge, and the legacy we leave behind—a canvas where we paint our stories, etching our presence into existence. On the other side, death emerges as the enigmatic realm awaiting every living being, a great equalizer indifferent to age, status, or achievements. It beckons introspection, prompting contemplation of the ephemeral nature of our earthly journey. The mystery surrounding what lies beyond adds an element of awe and uncertainty to the concept of death.

The interplay between life and death imparts meaning to our moments, urging us to cherish the present and discern purpose in our existence. It serves as a reminder that life's brevity imparts value to each breath, encouraging us to live authentically and leave a meaningful imprint on the world. In essence, life and death each bestow significance upon the other. The cyclical nature of existence, with its ebbs and flows, invites contemplation on the profound journey from the cradle to the inevitable embrace of the unknown.

From a psychological dynamic, the archetypal perspective on life and death delves into the profound symbolic patterns deeply rooted in the collective human psyche. These archetypes, recurring in myths, symbols, and cultural narratives, play a significant role in shaping our understanding of existence.

Within this psychological framework, life embodies the archetypal hero's journey. This narrative mirrors the psychological growth and transformation we undergo throughout our own lives. The call to adventure represents the initiation into life's challenges and experiences, echoing the universal quest for meaning, self-discovery, and the fulfillment of one's destiny.

The Hero's Journey

The hero's journey, as applied to life, signifies an ongoing cycle of birth, growth, and evolution. The trials, encounters with mentors, and battles against inner and outer challenges parallel the psychological processes of development, learning, and overcoming obstacles. The archetypal pattern reflects the human psyche's inherent drive for purpose and self-realization. Conversely, death is symbolized by archetypal figures such as the underworld. In the psychological realm, death is not merely a physical endpoint but a symbolic threshold representing the cyclical nature of life. This archetype suggests a transformative process, a journey into the unknown or descent into the underworld of the unconscious. Through this symbolic death, we confront deeper aspects of the self and undergo psychological rebirth or a new phase of existence.

The interplay between life and death in the psychological realm forms an archetypal duality—a symbolic dance embodying the eternal cycle of creation, destruction, and renewal within the human psyche. This dynamic serves as a metaphor for the psychological aspects of the human experience, underscoring the significance of embracing change, confronting psychological challenges, and recognizing the cyclical nature of personal growth and transformation. Cynthia Occelli depicts this reality flawlessly in her quote, "For a seed to achieve its greatest expression, it must come completely undone. The shell cracks, its insides come out and everything changes. To someone who doesn't understand growth, it would look like complete destruction."[10]

Essentially, the psychological interpretation of the archetypal perspective in the hero's journey invites us to perceive the hero's life as integral components of a broader narrative. This encourages a deeper psychological understanding of personal growth, the pursuit of psychological meaning, and the transformative psychological journey that extends beyond the confines of physical existence.

Regardless of our interpretation of the dichotomy between life and death, one undeniable truth emerges: Everyone, having entered this world, will eventually leave it. Throughout this journey, whether consciously or unconsciously, we undergo numerous psychological deaths and rebirths. When undertaken consciously, these processes not only bring more meaning to the journey, making pain more bearable, but also result in a greater sense of fulfillment and achievement of personal goals. Conversely, when we remain unconscious of these processes, we are merely thrust into the unpredictable currents of life, suffering through events

10 Cynthia Occelli, *Resurrecting Venus* (Agape Media, 2012)

and circumstances that persistently appear meaningless and render us as victims of circumstance.

When we set out on any journey—whether mastering a skill or navigating life itself—we often seek a sense of harmony that comes from combining knowledge with deeper understanding. This combination is what creates a meaningful and connected experience. Moving forward without self-awareness, however, can lead us to learn reactively, shaped by unplanned challenges or surprising encounters that test our ability to cope. Many people avoid facing these challenges directly, using distractions or self-sabotage to numb the discomfort. Psychologists explain that this avoidance may relieve stress temporarily, but it prevents true growth and self-discovery.

By choosing instead to approach our journey with openness and curiosity, we allow ourselves to gain valuable insights and build resilience. Facing life's challenges directly helps us grow emotionally, making it easier to interpret difficult experiences as opportunities for self-improvement. This mindset turns obstacles into valuable lessons, empowering us to live more authentically and with a sense of purpose.

Embracing Mortality Through a Harmonious Life Perspective

Developing a harmonious relationship with the cycle of life and death requires reflection on personal experiences, thoughts, and beliefs about existence and mortality. By exploring these reflections, you can cultivate a deeper understanding of life's transitions, drawing meaning from both the joys and sorrows that make up the human journey. Let's break down key areas for reflection and consider examples to help you engage with these concepts in a meaningful way.

To engage with the cycle of life and death, it's important to first reflect on what gives life meaning for you personally. What do you perceive as the essence of life? This might be tied to relationships, creativity, personal growth, or a deeper connection to the world around you. You may find that the core essence of life lies in your relationships with loved ones and your ability to contribute positively to your community. As you reflect on this, you might realize that your purpose is rooted in fostering meaningful connections and leaving a legacy of kindness. Understanding this essence helps ground your approach to life and how you navigate difficult times.

Your perspective on death deeply influences how you live. Consider how you perceive the end of life—whether as a finality or a transition to something else. Understanding your relationship with death can help you cultivate acceptance and peace as part of life's natural cycle. Someone who views death as a transition may find solace in spiritual beliefs or the idea of continuing influence through memories and legacies. By contemplating death as a natural part of life's journey, they might engage in practices like meditation or writing letters to loved ones to process emotions and cultivate peace about their own mortality.

Nature's cycles offer profound wisdom for understanding the ebb and flow of life. Reflecting on the seasons, growth, decay, and renewal in the natural world can mirror the transitions in your own life and provide insights into embracing change. Observing the cycles of nature—such as the way trees shed leaves in autumn only to bloom again in spring—can remind someone that life has its seasons of loss and renewal. When facing personal challenges, this perspective can encourage them to trust in the natural process of life, knowing that after difficult periods, new growth will emerge.

Part of building a harmonious relationship with life and death involves honoring those who have passed. Consider how you keep the memory of loved ones alive through rituals, reflection, or daily practices that carry their legacy forward. An individual might light a candle each year on the anniversary of a loved one's passing or create a memory book that captures cherished moments. By doing this, they honor the life of those who have passed while acknowledging their ongoing presence in their heart and life.

Acceptance is key to navigating life's inevitable changes. Reflect on how you practice acceptance when faced with uncertainty or major life transitions, and how this acceptance helps you approach these moments with grace. Someone who has experienced a significant career change might reflect on how accepting the situation allowed them to let go of resistance and approach the new opportunity with an open mind. By embracing the transition instead of fearing it, they found new pathways to growth and fulfillment.

Both joy and sorrow are integral parts of life, and finding meaning in each can help you develop a balanced, more profound appreciation of your journey. Reflect on how these experiences shape your understanding of life's purpose. A person who has gone through the highs of love and the pain of loss might reflect on how each has deepened their emotional capacity. By acknowledging that both joy and sorrow have contributed to their emotional and spiritual growth, they find greater meaning in their journey, embracing life's complexity rather than avoiding its challenges.

When thinking about the cycle of life and death, consider the legacy you want to leave behind. This isn't just about material success, but the values, contributions, and impact you wish to have on the world and the people around you. Someone who values education and community-building might spend time mentoring young people or creating a community project. By aligning their actions with the legacy they want to leave, they ensure that their life reflects their deepest values and creates a lasting positive impact, even beyond their own lifespan.

Gratitude can dramatically shift how you view both life and death. By focusing on what you are grateful for, you can develop a sense of peace about life's impermanence and embrace the present moment more fully. Someone might practice gratitude each morning by reflecting on the simple joys of life—their health, a sunrise, the love of friends and family. By incorporating gratitude into their daily routine, they cultivate a mindset that celebrates life and helps ease anxieties about death, viewing it as a natural conclusion to a life well-lived.

Compassion toward yourself and others is essential during times of transition. Reflect on how you show kindness during moments of change and how that compassion eases the emotional strain of navigating life's challenges. During a personal loss, an individual might consciously offer themselves patience and understanding, refraining from harsh self-criticism. They may also extend that compassion to family members by offering support without judgment. This mindset of kindness fosters emotional resilience and encourages healing during periods of transition.

Reflecting on the interconnectedness of life helps you understand that death is not a solitary event but part of a larger tapestry of existence. Recognizing your role in this interconnected web can bring a sense of unity and peace when contemplating mortality. Someone who gardens might see themselves as part of the natural cycle, knowing that the plants they nurture will one day die, return to the earth, and contribute to future growth. This perspective helps them understand that life and death are not separate but deeply intertwined, fostering a sense of belonging to the larger cycle of existence.

By engaging with these reflections, we begin to see life and death as parts of a larger, interconnected cycle. Embracing both the joys and the challenges allows us to approach our journey with acceptance, gratitude, and a sense of purpose. The more we explore and understand our own perspectives on existence, the more equipped we are to face life's transitions with grace and resilience. In doing so, we cultivate a harmonious relationship with ourselves and the world around us—finding peace in the knowledge that every experience, whether of loss or growth, contributes to the tapestry of a life well-lived.

Conclusion

A New Beginning

As we near the conclusion of this transformative journey of self-discovery, we find ourselves not at a destination but at a new beginning. The path we've walked has been adorned with moments of revelation, introspection, and profound growth, each step guiding us closer to the essence of our being.

In the intricate mosaic of our lives, we've unraveled threads of self-awareness, resilience, and authenticity. We've confronted fears, embraced strengths, and navigated the nuances of our inner world with courage and compassion.

This expedition of self-discovery hasn't been devoid of challenges. We've encountered uncertainty, self-doubt, and moments of discomfort as we confronted shadows and unveiled buried truths. Yet through these trials, we've unearthed the transformative potential of vulnerability and self-acceptance.

As we draw this chapter of exploration to a close, we carry with us a newfound clarity, purpose, and inner equilibrium. We've realized that self-discovery isn't a fixed point but an ongoing journey, a continual peeling back of layers and discoveries that enrich the tapestry of our existence.

May we perpetuate a spirit of curiosity, openness, and self-reflection as we navigate life's evolving landscape. Let us honor our journey by honoring ourselves, embracing our authenticity, and living with intention and meaning.

In celebration of the profound alchemy of self-discovery, let us embark on each new day with gratitude, courage, and a heart filled with the boundless possibilities of our true selves.

About the Author

Dr. Shahrzad Jalali, known to her clients as Dr. Jalali, is a clinical psychologist and trauma specialist whose work is rooted in psychoanalysis and trauma-informed care. With a unique approach that integrates somatic and bottom-up methods, she invites her readers to go beyond conventional therapeutic boundaries, encouraging a deeper connection to both mind and body.

Dr. Jalali's own journey of healing from trauma profoundly shapes her insights, lending an authenticity and warmth that resonates with those she supports. Her practice and teachings center on helping individuals explore the complexities of the human psyche, revealing paths to resilience and wholeness.

As a thought leader, Dr. Jalali has built a robust presence, connecting with a diverse audience and sharing valuable perspectives on mental health. She believes that by learning to tame and integrate the psyche, one can actively shape life's course and align it with true desires. Conversely, when the psyche is left unexamined, it has the power to control, rendering one vulnerable to life's circumstances.

Her work extends beyond the therapy room, where she mentors emerging professionals in the field, guiding them to approach mental health with both depth and compassion. Through her teachings and mentorship, Dr. Jalali inspires a new generation of practitioners to embrace a holistic, trauma-informed approach to healing.